NOTES FROM
THE BOTTOM
OF THE WORLD

NOTES FROM THE BOTTOM OF THE WORLD

A Life in Chile

SUZANNE ADAM

She Writes Press, a BookSparks imprint
A Division of SparkPointStudio, LLC.

Published 2018

Printed in the United States of America

978-1-63152-415-8 paperback
978-1-63152-416-5 ebook
Library of Congress Control Number: 2018957312

For information, address:
She Writes Press
1569 Solano Ave #546
Berkeley, CA 94707

She Writes Press is a division of SparkPoint Studio, LLC.

All company and/or product names may be trade names, logos, trademarks, and/or registered trademarks and are the property of their respective owners.

Names and identifying characteristics have been changed to protect the privacy of certain individuals.

The essay *Fishing Lessons* was first published in the November 8, 2009, issue of the *Christian Science Monitor.*

A version of *The Morning With Oscar* was first published in the *Christian Science Monitor,* May 30, 2011.

Sins of Omission was first published in the winter issue of *Persimmon Tree,* 2015.

A version of *The Fox and His Rose* won a Judge's Special Award in the 2012 Past Loves Day Story Contest.

CONTENTS

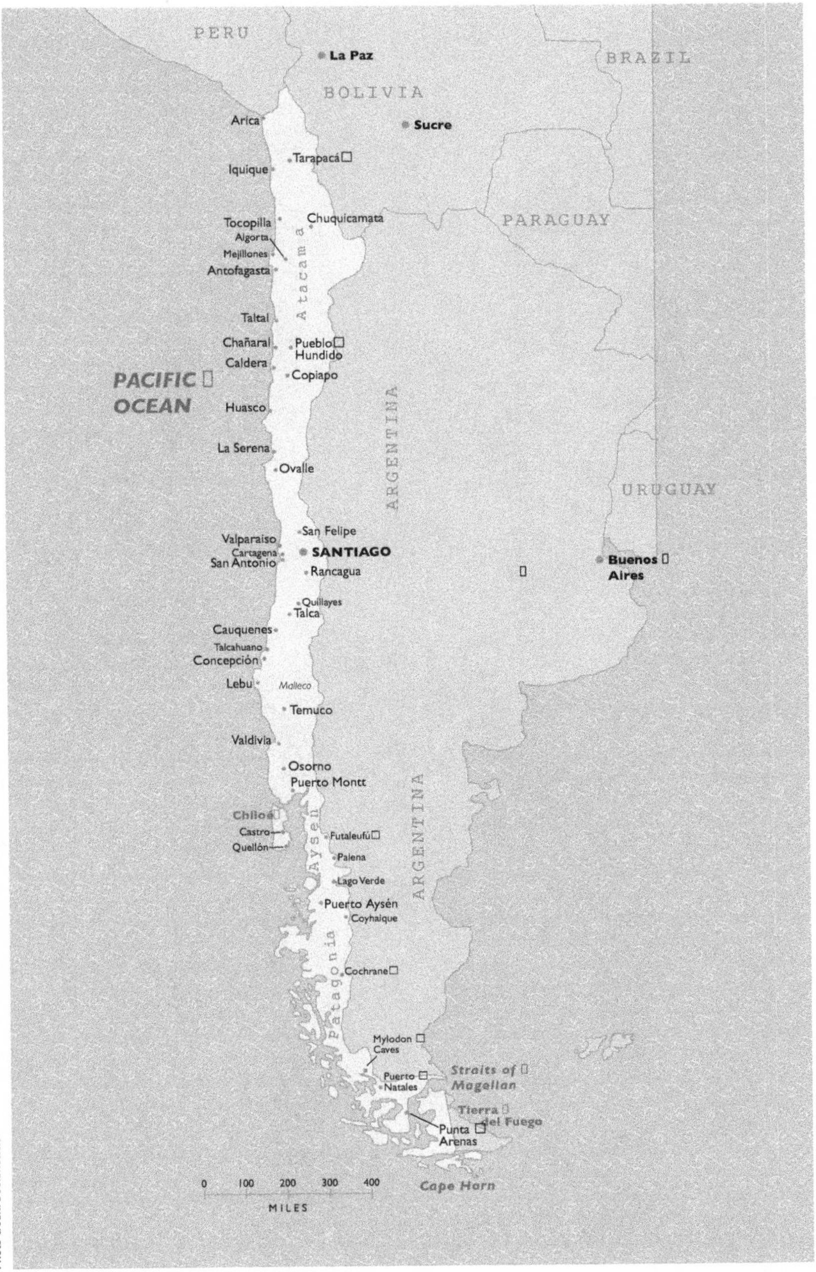

Photo credit: BookMatters

I. AMERICAN ROOTS

I've lived a greater portion of my life in Chile than in the States, yet my connection with my homeland remains strong. I often recall Wallace Stegner's thoughts on the subject: "Whatever landscape a child is exposed to early on, that will be the sort of gauze through which he or she will see the world afterwards."

Ghosts of High School Past

Santiago, Chile, 2009

Curious, I click on the bright blue letters. "Welcome to the class of 1960 web page." A former classmate sent me the link. The announcement continues, "Believe it or not, plans are in the works for our fiftieth high school reunion in 2010."

Fifty years.

I've kept in touch with only two classmates. My friend Carole writes that she's not planning to go. Me neither, I reply. I've never gone to a high school reunion. Why go now? My date to the senior ball invited me to the fifth reunion, but I declined. I had a boyfriend and no interest in looking backward. High school was a closed chapter in my life. I'd exchanged my hometown friends for the wide world of Berkeley. After I moved to Chile in 1972, an unreliable mail system, no telephone, and, for decades, no Internet made keeping in touch difficult.

In high school we shy ones were tender green shoots, vulnerable and insecure. It was an era of cliques, popularity pecking orders, and unrequited love. I had a crush on Chuck. So did half the girls in class. A couple of cool, crew-cut seniors were also the objects of my romantic longings, that painful teenage propensity for impossible love. Years later, one of them became US poet laureate. At least I had good taste.

On the website class list of 186 names, sixteen are tagged with a rose, signifying that they are deceased. I read the biographies. Two suicides. One Vietnam fatality. I click on other names—friends, meanies, nerds, the cheerleader crowd. A few have courageously sent recent photos. I rush to examine myself in the mirror. Do I look that old?

What the heck. I click on my name and write a brief biography in the space provided, carefully wording it to make the best possible impression. My prophecy in the senior yearbook predicted I'd be an efficiency expert, but I want to show that my life has been far from dull. The shy adolescent lurking within wants to project a confident, mature woman. I punch SEND.

The next day, an email pops up from Missy, my classmate at St. Anselm's Grammar School and my Girl Scouts buddy. More emails follow, one from a fellow I've known since the first grade. My high school self-image is shaken. We must have selective memories of those fragile years. Maybe others perceive or remember us differently than we do ourselves. If these people took the time to write, maybe I'm not a nerd after all.

Will I go? I feel like Peggy Sue from the Coppola film. But, unlike her, I can't rewrite the past, and I worry that revisiting it might distract me from living fully in the present. Yet, lately, there's an itch in me to come full circle, tie up loose ends, look up old flames. I update family photo albums, complete my family tree, and Google the names of long-lost friends. Should I risk facing the old ghosts of high school insecurity? Does it matter now?

I check out more photos on the web page: classmates, spouses, kids, grandkids. They look like interesting, amiable people that I'd like to get to know. I've a year to decide. Soon I'll be making my yearly visit back to my hometown of San Anselmo, California. Three of us are planning lunch—a dry run for the reunion, a test of self-confidence for a once awkward high school girl.

Months later, I walk into the Cheesecake Factory and look around. A redhead waves at me from a booth. It's Melodie, and next to her is Carole. We hug and look each other over. I haven't seen them since high school graduation, though we've been in touch the past year by email. Our talk is nonstop: of children (each of us has two boys), grandchildren, jobs, travels. Then we naturally move on to discuss classmates. Here, I'm at a disadvantage, having been out of touch for decades, although the biographies on the class website have helped bring me up to date.

"How are the reunion plans coming along?" I ask Melodie. She and her husband, Joe, are the main organizers.

"Good. We have an official reunion committee now. But I guess you've read Missy's objections to the place and time. She's become a real pain. Disagrees with everything. We've decided to ignore her comments."

I have read Missy's lengthy entries on the website. Besides disagreeing with reunion details, she wrote long missives about her life, her abusive father, her marriage to a Hollywood producer, her divorce, her diabetes, and her return to our home county. Her stories, as well as her personal emails, have convinced me that she possesses a very creative imagination. One story I choose to believe is how my mother, our Girl Scout leader, brought Missy to our house to help her finish the requirements for Girl Scout badges, all of which Missy wanted to earn. My mother told me a few years ago that she believed Missy was a neglected child. At St. Anselm's, Missy was a sprightly, blond-headed girl who often got into trouble with the nuns. Once, she cut a hole in her school uniform, which usually looked unironed.

I arrange to meet her for lunch at a restaurant in San Anselmo. The sight of her heavy, big-bosomed figure and thin, long hair is a shock. Her face is so changed, I would not have recognized her on the street. Her speech is slurred because of ill-fitting dentures.

Poor Missy. She's made several enemies among her old class-mates. I choose to ignore the feud, this time thankful for the geographical distance. She continues to write me, complaining when I don't answer immediately. She and Carole have a fall-ing-out over the same issue. I tell her that I email many friends and that she mustn't think I don't love her. She writes about her new plants for her patio and sends me a catalog of garden seeds. Missy needs friendship, and I'm happy to be there for her—at a distance.

"I'm not going to the reunion," she confides. "I tried to help with the organization, but people were really nasty to me. Are you going?"

"Yes, I've decided to go. I've never attended a class reunion, so fifty seems like a good number."

Back to School Days

Marin County, California, 2010

Did I really go to school with these people? We're no longer the seventeen-year-olds portrayed in the senior-year photos on our name tags. It's as if Time, that old trickster, has pressed the fast-forward button on the fifty-year-old high school reel.

I ponder possible reasons that motivated me to come to this reunion: the desire to reconnect with friends from my youth; curiosity; a subconscious wish to reunite with my childhood self; my decades-long nostalgia for home. I've traveled from Santiago, Chile, where I've lived for thirty-eight years. I don't know what to expect.

Over the phone, Karen, my neighborhood playmate and classmate since the first grade, suggests we go together to the Friday-night meet-and-greet event. Good. I need moral support. We agree to get together first over coffee at Barnes & Noble.

When I arrive, I hear someone call out, "Suzie?" It's Karen, shorter than I remember, with spiky blond hair. We hug and look each other over. We can't agree on when we last saw each other, at least twenty years ago. Our time is short, and we pour out confidences, making up for lost time.

At the meet-and-greet, I struggle to recognize former classmates in the sea of faces. Here's Carole. She's chatting with . . . Seeing my puzzled face, she says, "Remember Joe?"

I move amid the animated crowd. *Who are you? I'm . . . You've changed! You look the same! Whatever happened to . . . ?*

Unlike me, many of my classmates have stayed in touch over the years. I feel like the new kid at school. But everyone is friendly. We mingle, chat, and laugh. I come away with a good feeling and look forward to the dinner the next evening.

Saturday night. I've had my hair done and wear my slinky black dress. In the dining room, I look about for a spot with familiar faces. There's Karen, but her table is filled. Members of old cliques sit together, both gals and guys. I locate a place where my friends Carole and Joanne are seated. The others at the table weren't my close friends, and I'm disappointed, not enthused, by the idea of spending the entire evening with them. It's like meeting some of these women for the first time. But, as we talk, I find their stories interesting. We have taken such varied roads.

After dinner, there are prizes. No surprise that I win the one for having traveled the farthest. When the music starts, people stand to dance, visit other tables, and snap photos. Fifties songs form the backdrop of our reminiscing. When I hear the opening bars of "Rock Around the Clock," I sway, tap my foot, and call to Janice and Joanne, "Hey, come on. Let's dance!" This is no high-school sock hop, and I refuse to relive the wallflower experience. Janice, glowing in her glittery sequined jacket, jumps up. Quiet Joanne is reluctant, but I remind her, "Girls danced together in the fifties," and we join the other rock-and-rollers.

Later, I bump into Paul in the hallway. He says, "I'm sorry. I don't remember your name."

I tell him who I am and add, "Paul! We went to the Senior Ball together!"

"Oh! Sorry. You've changed."

The physical changes in faces and bodies shock, especially those of the men, as I didn't know any of my male classmates well. Ours was a Catholic high school, and most classes were segregated. Beards, fuller faces, and extra pounds make some difficult to place. Others I recognize immediately, handsome as ever. But it's not just the packaging that's different. Many greet me with warmth, validating the grown-up me. Barbara says she remembers me as a calm girl with beautiful handwriting. *Lord, I hope I'll be remembered for something more than my penmanship.* Karen recalls the time our Brownie troop went to a pool where she almost drowned. I jumped in to save her but landed on top of her. A true friend. I'm disappointed that others, who were once my friends, don't bother to come to talk and that, even now, I'm too shy to break into their circles of conversation.

My Chile connection prompts some to ask, "Were you there when the miners were rescued? It was so moving."

Doug comes up and tells me about his trip to Chile.

"When were you in Chile?"

His face lights up as he describes visiting wineries and climbing the steep steps of Valparaiso.

"You know, Doug," I laugh, "I don't think we spoke even four words in high school!"

Later in the evening, I locate Karen's petite figure across the room. "I wish we'd had more time to talk," I tell her. We hug goodbye and exchange email addresses, promising to keep in touch. She lives in Arkansas now. Crossing paths again won't be easy.

In spite of the distance and the years, I still care about these people. Remembering my sixteen deceased classmates, I'm sharply aware of my mortality. I believe we all are. Yes, we've aged, but we take comfort in knowing we're not alone. This reunion is a celebration of life among the friends with whom we shared those fragile days of youth. Several of those friendships hark back to St. Anselm's Elementary School. Reconnecting with them triggers vivid early childhood memories: old Monsignor

McGarr's lengthy gospels, my swing under the cypress tree, fishing with my father, the scent of roses in my maternal grandmother's garden, Girl Scout camping days at Huckleberry Woods. Though we all have recollections we'd rather forget, I choose to focus on the good memories that bring me immense pleasure, a delight that intensifies as I reminisce with old friends who lived those same experiences.

Swing

The first swing my father made for me was an old rubber tire suspended by a rope from a thick branch of the cypress tree. Later it was followed by a board held by two scratchy ropes, again in the shade of the old cypress. There I learned to pump, thrusting my legs forward and then bending them back. Learning to pump meant I was grown-up—five or six. At St. Anselm's school playground, I competed with others. Who could fly the highest? The playground swings hung from a bar on heavy metal chains that squeaked and clanked as I soared higher and higher. Soon I could even jump off while still in motion, landing firmly on my feet.

Later, swings became child's play and I was off to another section of the playground to play kickball, volleyball, and softball. A strong batter, I loved the cracking sound as the wooden bat connected with the ball. But while I was wielding the bat, another swing burst into my life: rock and roll.

When I was eleven or twelve, I rocked to Jerry Lee Lewis and Fats Domino with boys shorter than I, their eyes level with my budding breasts. Better yet, I swung with my best friend Karen in my living room to our favourite 45s: Buddy Holly's "That'll Be the Day" and Ray Charles's "What'd I Say."

That was then. Now, in my kitchen, I wiggle my hips to Aretha and James Brown on the radio. And I take my twin granddaughters, Colomba and Manuela, to the plaza where they call me to watch how they've learned to pump their little legs. There's an empty swing next to them. I sit down and push off, thrusting my legs forward and back. Harder and harder. Higher. Higher. Reaching for the sky. Hair flying, the wind brushing my face. Laughing. The girls and I.

Fishing Lessons

My father's only child, I was the obvious candidate to be his fishing companion. He taught me to bait a hook, cast and reel in, play the fish to tire it, and then gut and clean my catch.

My most vivid memories of our fishing outings are of those at Lily Lake in the Sierra Nevada Mountains. By age six, I'd learned lesson number one in fish behavior: they liked an early breakfast, which meant crawling from our sleeping bags before dawn. In our clunky Plymouth, we climbed the winding road to the lake. Holding on to a waist-high wire, we crossed Glen Alpine Creek's wooden-slat footbridge, built atop a beaver dam. A path led us to the boat, tied up at the water's edge.

My father rowed us through the dark green channels among the lily pads. We spoke softly, the only other sounds the liquid dipping of the oars or an occasional bird cry. Choosing a promising-looking spot, he'd rustle through his tackle box among sinkers, spools of nylon line, fishing flies, and cans of worms, searching for hooks and weights. We baited our hooks, cast our lines, and waited. For those few hours, the little lake was ours.

My father and I had an uneasy relationship. I was an introverted child around him. He and my mother bickered constantly, and he had a drinking problem. His behavior too often embarrassed me. But on those fishing mornings, there was no bottle hidden in his jacket, no slurred speech, no glazed eyes. I felt safe with our fishermen's talk. There, my father was on his own turf. He could teach me the lessons of fishing—not only the how-tos, but other lessons he didn't know he was imparting to me:

We don't always get what we came for.
With patience, though, we might.
The wait can be as satisfying as the reward.
Much can be heard in the quiet of the dawn.
Silences between two people don't need to be filled.

Sometimes a foolish trout found my hook. I'd reel it in, and my father would scoop it out with his net. We estimated its length, admiring its identifying markings. He'd remove the hook and give the fish a quick blow on the head.

When the fish had eaten their fill, we rowed back to shore and headed to camp, where my mother waited with a welcome breakfast. I don't remember how old I was the last time I went fishing with my father at Lily Lake. Eventually, I became more interested in snaring boys. But those fishing times were the closest moments I had with him as a child.

My father is gone now, but I returned recently to Lily Lake. I crossed the wooden footbridge and stood on the shore. A silver flash broke the water's placid surface, spreading glistening concentric rings. I was there again with my father, rowing through islands of lily pads, and I whispered a *thank you* for what he'd taught me.

Knickerbockers

In the black-and-white photograph my father looks to be about seven years old. He's wearing long, dark socks under wool knickerbockers, a big-collared shirt with a wide tie, a pullover sweater, and a jockey cap. I suppose he's dressed in the fashion of the times, the early 1920s. My grandmother undoubtedly chose the outfit for him. He looks as if he just stepped off the pages of a Hardy Boys book or out of a scene from *The Little Rascals*.

Though not a vain man, as he aged, my father began to give more attention to his clothes. When he dressed to go out, he looked positively dapper. In winter he'd wear a wool cap similar to the one in the photo. I can picture him in the hall, pulling on a camel-colored sweater over an attractive sport shirt and matching pants and shoes. He lost weight in his later years and cut a fine figure. His thick black hair was now a salt-and-pepper gray, which he wore in a stylish cut. The finishing touch was a gold coin on a chain around his neck.

This keen interest in his clothes and appearance took me by surprise. I no longer lived at home so hadn't observed the process. Remembering the photo of him as a boy, I wonder if his interest in clothes had always been there and resurfaced at a time in his life when he'd started taking better care of himself, a wiser man who had learned to control what he ate and drank. A man who had finally learned to love himself.

Faith Journey

As students at St. Anselm's School in the 1950s, we attended Sunday Mass, singing portions of Gregorian chant, accompanied by the pipe organ. *Agnus Dei, qui tollis peccáta mundi . . .* We followed the Latin text in booklets, though years of repetition soon rendered the text superfluous.

Our class sat together, we girls, heads covered, behind the boys in separate pews, which gave us an excellent view of the back of Eddie McGraw's head, sporting his divine crew cut. If we were lucky, we wouldn't be stuck behind Bobby Brady's pimply neck and greasy hair. Black-and-white-habited Sister Josephine Mary, perched by the center aisle, kept us in line like a bookend. I swore she saw through the starched wimple framing her face, sending us piercing looks at the slightest whisper. If someone giggled, muffled laughs and snorts followed in a chain reaction. Careful. Sister might make one of us sit next to her.

The Gospel. Sister pulled her wooden, castanet-like clapper from a deep pocket of her long black habit and signaled. *Clack.* Stand. Old Monsignor McGarr intoned the monophonic plainchant—*Dóminus vobíscum,* the Lord be with you—and we'd reply, *Et cum spíritu tuo.* After the Gospel, *clack.* Sit for the sermon. Tuning out his droning voice, I'd often think about our neighbor's bomb shelter down the block and, gazing toward the statue of the virgin, flickering with votive candles, say a prayer for peace with Russia. Mostly, though, I'd watch the boys wriggling and smirking. Mike Carter was almost as cute as Eddie McGraw.

When I was eleven, I began taking my own St. Joseph Daily Missal to church. Turning the sheer, gold-edged pages, I would follow the Mass in Latin and English. I also learned the names of the layers of the priest's vestments and the liturgical colors he would wear that day. In spite of my devout intentions—I toyed with the idea of missionary work in Africa—a High Mass, celebrated by three priests, followed by the recitation of a litany, tested my resolve. Yet I faithfully repeated "pray for us" after each poetic, soothingly repetitious line. *Mary, Mirror of Justice, pray for us; Throne of Wisdom, pray for us; Glory of Israel, pray for us; Mystical Rose, pray for us; Morning Star, pray for us.*

Once in high school, I no longer attended the children's Mass. A conscientious student, in religion class I memorized lists of sacraments, types of grace, and categories of sin. I examined my conscience and confessed to having impure thoughts and disobeying my parents. My one rebellious act was not heeding the nuns' warnings to choose a Catholic college, lest, out in the secular world, we lose our faith. But I'd made up my mind. The world of Berkeley and its university beckoned.

There, I first became aware of being *Catholic*, a member of a minority. Sundays I would make my way across campus to the Newman Catholic Center, where, in an open, joyful environment, freed from the sternness of the past, I began to discover my own spirituality. Accompanied by guitars, we clapped and sang the "amen" chorus from Sidney Poitier's movie *Lilies of the Field*. No more Latin. Seldom the scent of incense.

Berkeley wasn't what propelled me into that shady category, a fallen-away Catholic. It was my years of Peace Corps service that made me a doubting Thomas. In the Colombian barrio where I worked, bald Padre Andrés, clad in a long white cassock, chided those of his flock who lived in sin with their mates, which was most of them. I questioned what constituted sin for people who inhabited one-room shacks, the entire family sleeping in one bed. Ester, my neighbor next door, asked me for money for an abortion. I couldn't turn my back on her and her five little boys, whose big brown eyes and distended bellies spoke of hunger.

Having my own children brought me back to the Church. Wanting to raise our two boys, Daniel and Nicolas, in the faith, my husband, Santiago, and I knew we would have to be their role models. I never recovered the unquestioning faith of my childhood. I've learned that faith requires daily renewal, and that rituals, while beautiful, are not the only paths to a prayerful state of mind. Nicolas, our younger son, now no longer a churchgoer, told me, "Nature is my cathedral." He became aware of this much earlier than I did.

Santiago and I were fortunate that we shared a common faith. Starting our life together, we still had to negotiate our country of residence, our home language, schools for our children. Our initial plan was to wed in Chile and then move to California. But plans often change.

Finding Myself in the Beats

My son Danny, returned to Chile from an exchange semester at Berkeley, had treated me to a recitation of Beat poet Allen Ginsberg's "Hadda Be Playin' on the Jukebox." Robert Hass's American Poetry class had introduced Danny to the Beats, and he wanted to know whether I'd read Jack Kerouac's *On the Road*. I hadn't.

Suddenly I was aware of a gaping hole in my education, and in my coolness. I had missed the Beats. I was a Berkeley graduate and grew up in the Bay Area in the 1950s and 60s, when the Beats burst onto the scene. How did it all pass me by?

As a naive high school senior, I attended an event for prospective majors at the University of California's speech department, where I heard a recording of Lawrence Ferlinghetti reading his poetry. What I understood of the poem—something about a white snake, which I guessed was a phallic symbol—turned my ears a searing scarlet. The Beats' rages against the establishment held little interest for this conventional girl, product of twelve years of Catholic education. I decided to major in political science.

Now, at the age of sixty-nine, with Danny's copy of *On the Road* in hand, I want to see how I react to it. American road-trip tales lure me—John Steinbeck's *Travels with Charley*, William Least Heat-Moon's *Blue Highways*—and quench my thirst for home. Where will Kerouac's road trip take me?

As narrator Sal Paradise begins his westward wanderings, I'm drawn to his fascination with the American landscape, his obsession with the *idea* of America, its vastness, its geography. He notices what I'd notice: a sunrise and dew, clouds and gopher holes, cactus and mesquite. His journeys pulsate with the American places that come to mind when I imagine crossing the land I left over forty years ago to live in Chile: dilapidated gas stations, bus depots, diners with winking neon signs, pastel-colored suburban houses.

I nod and smile when Sal reaches San Francisco to encounter the daunting steep streets and haunting moans of nighttime foghorns. My early childhood flickers into view. My father, a San Francisco native, wore badge 498 of the city's police department and patrolled undercover the streets of Chinatown, where I attended day care.

Sal hangs out with the people who slept, loved, and worked in these places: tired blond waitresses, hobos, "broken-down movie extras," bellhops, old miners—emblematic, sentimentalized figures, but part of the nation's idea of itself.

Who were these wild people upon whom Kerouac based his characters? The Internet introduces me to his pals Neal Cassady, Allen Ginsberg, and Lawrence Ferlinghetti.

I scour Ferlinghetti's works for the scandalous poem. None is familiar. This time, rather than being shocked, I'm surprised at the poems' clarity and relevance. "Bird with Two Right Wings" should be required reading in a US presidential election year.

A distant memory of my father surfaces as I read about the 1957 trial in which Ferlinghetti was charged with selling obscene material—Ginsberg's book *Howl and Other Poems*—in his City Lights bookstore. I recall my father telling of his involvement in an obscenity trial. Which trial? I hunt for answers. In a photo album I find a yellowed newspaper clipping with a front-page photograph of my dad, special investigator for the Marin County district attorney. Three years after the *Howl* case, he bought Henry Miller's *Tropic of Cancer* from a local bookseller as evidence for an upcoming obscenity trial. As in the *Howl* case, Henry Miller's book was not ruled obscene. All this going on right under my nose!

Now more versed in the Beats' works, I realize how deeply they influenced my generation. We were Kennedy-era, romantic idealists who dared to question authority—war, segregation, plundering of the planet. Though the Beats' erratic lives couldn't have been more different from my own, I understand their insatiable appetite for life, for knowing, their search for *it*.

Despite the generation gap, my son and I can now discuss these works.

Yet, even with Kerouac in hand, I find that the knowledge gap widens daily. This road has no final destination.

But what a trip.

Now, where in Chile can I get a copy of *Trópico de Cáncer* in English?

I don't have to look far. Danny lends me his copy. Henry Miller's stream-of-consciousness style puts me off, and his low life and sexual exploits in 1930s Paris do not grab my interest. I return the book to Danny. At loose ends for something to read, I turn to the Brainpickings website, which abounds with names of books and writers. An article referring to the wit and intelligence of Ursula K. Le Guin's essay collection *The Wave of the Mind* sparks my curiosity. Her name sounds familiar.

Literary Muses

Who is Ursula Le Guin? I turn to the Internet, where several surprises await me. Familiar names and places. She grew up in Berkeley, where I lived for eight years, though our time there didn't coincide. She was the daughter of Alfred and Theodora Kroeber, renowned anthropologists, her father the director of the university's anthropology museum. Theodora wrote one of my most-loved books, *Ishi in Two Worlds*, an account of the last Native American living in the wilderness of California. I first read the book as a student in Berkeley soon after its publication, in 1961.

These coincidences (or maybe serendipity?) prompt me to explore more about Ursula Le Guin. Her novels are classified as fantasy/science fiction, genres that have never appealed to me. None of the titles sound familiar, but their descriptions spark my curiosity. Maybe it's time for this reader to branch out.

I spend an hour browsing her blog, which she continues to maintain in her eighties. Funny, entertaining, thought-provoking, she describes her cat's antics, shoots darts at book publishers and consumer-based capitalism, and talks tough and personally about aging. Blog post number sixty-nine, "The Diminished Thing," is profound. She approaches with dry humor the common negative attitudes of the younger generations toward aging and the aged, while exploring the positive realities of "geezerhood" (rich old intelligence, the gift of time) and the frustrations of breakdowns in the body (less mobility and strength, memory slippage). I hear you, Ursula.

Although always a reader, I came to the writing craft late in life. Ursula shows me that older women have much of value to say at this stage in life, when it is so easy to feel irrelevant and diminished. I can almost hear her tell me, *Fiddlesticks! Of course people will be interested in what you have to say.* In fact, she'd probably use a stronger word than "fiddlesticks." When my head goes blank while searching for a blog topic, I look at her wide range of themes, from the academic (her fifty favorite books) to the personal (her dislike of flying), which encourages me to think, *I can do that, too!* When she refers to her "crabby old age," I feel liberated. *Yes! It's okay to feel crabby when I count out the eight pills I must swallow each morning or trip over the vacuum cord.*

She is now my mentor, my muse, and my model. I want to challenge myself and read one of her science-fiction novels, but first I borrow back my yellowed copy of *Ishi in Two Worlds* from Danny, who has also taken an interest in Native Americans.

I have never lost my love for California's early history. The story of the extermination of Northern California's Yana tribe and Ishi's subgroup, the Yahi, by local ranchers is deeply disturbing. The names and explicit details bring events to life, taking me to Yahi tribal lands—to Mule and Deer Creeks and the rugged foothills of Mt. Lassen, where I camped as a child. I know the territory.

Two anthropologists, Thomas Waterman and Alfred Kroeber, introduced Ishi into modern society. They, in contrast with the ranchers, recognized Ishi's uniqueness, his gentleness and worth. Waterman and Kroeber became his close friends, along with Dr. Saxton Pope, a member of the university medical school staff.

Ishi went on to become a research assistant at the museum, then located in San Francisco. With low resistance to "diseases of civilization," he suffered ill health, spending much time in the university hospital, where my great-aunt Anne, a student nurse, met him. How I wish I'd asked her about her experience. But then I was young and lacked the foresight to ask the older generations in my family about their stories.

Ishi's story has moments of joy. I imagine his immense contentment, though mixed with sadness, when he returns to his beloved homeland with his three white friends, where they camp and live as Ishi's Yahi tribe once did, subsisting off the land, shooting game, and spearing fish. Now *he* is their teacher.

Ishi is given free rein to wander about his museum-home and the medical school, where, as his English skills improve, he visits with hospital staff, nurses, doctors, janitors, and patients. Did my great-aunt Anne talk to him? Treat him during his hospital stays? Looking for answers, I pull out her album of black-and-white photographs, glued firmly to the thick black paper used in those years.

Young student nurses, clad in high-necked, long uniforms with full white pinafores and white caps, pose on the steps of the medical center on Parnassus Heights. I recognize the tall one as my great-aunt. In one picture, they wear white masks and attend a patient on a surgical table. In another, they pose holding quadruplets. Sadly, my aunt did not label her photographs. One of a bespectacled man, clad in a surgical gown, sitting at a desk, arouses my curiosity. I Google Dr. Saxton Pope ("Popey" to Ishi) and compare photos. Yes, that's him, Ishi's dear friend and archery companion. Excited by my discovery, I write under the photo, in silver ink, "Dr. Saxton Pope, friend of Ishi's." I find no photos of Ishi.

A pall of sadness descends as I read the last pages of *Ishi* and its chronicle of his final days, in the University of California Anthropology Museum in San Francisco. In March 1916, just over one hundred years ago, he succumbed to tuberculosis. The grief of his three closest friends is now my grief. (Wikipedia notes that the museum was located in San Francisco from 1903 until 1931, when it moved to the campus of the University of California, Berkeley.)

My great-aunt worked for a time among a tribe of Northern Californian Native Americans. The only clues in her album are three photos of native families. Was it her contact with Ishi that prompted her to seek work with them? I wish I knew the name of the tribe that gave her the white patchwork quilt with green conifers, now among the family treasures I brought here to Chile.

When Danny came to lunch one day, I told him I was rereading *Ishi*.

"Do you remember much of it?" I ask. "The first part was about the massacre of Ishi's people."

"Just like what happened here in southern Chile with the native people."

I showed him my great-aunt's album, pointing out the photos I'd labeled. How many busy forty-year-old men want to look at one-hundred-year-old family photographs? Yet, to my pleasure, he was interested.

"I want you to know the stories," I tell him. "Someday you and Nico will have to sort through all our accumulations. It will be up to the two of you to pass on the narrative legacy of the American side of our family." Though these small stories are uniquely ours, I'm inclined to think that most of humankind's history is made up of myriad small stories.

Leaving California's past, I now venture into the futuristic world of Ursula's science-fiction novel *The Lathe of Heaven*. The plot evolves on dual time tracks and in alternate universes, leaving me perplexed. Ms. Le Guin published the book in 1971, while the actual present of the story seems to occur in the early part of the second millennium, thus being in my past. Tenuous, permeable lines distinguish between present, past, and future. This starts me wondering about time. The present is now the past as I write, yet it was once the future.

The story overwhelms with a plethora of man-made disasters: pollution, the greenhouse effect, continuous wars, overpopulation, famine, and riots; and natural disasters: volcanic eruptions, plagues. It's frightening to accept that this scenario *is* our recent past *and* our present. What a brilliant mind Le Guin has, to have created such a complex alternative reality that actually foreshadows her not-so-distant future. She manages to stretch my mind and imagination into untried territories.

Ursula Le Guin passed away January 24, 2018, at age eighty-eight.

Adventures with Gabriel

Now I make a leap from Ursula Le Guin's futuristic world into Gabriel García Márquez's phantasmagoric realm of magic realism in his *One Hundred Years of Solitude*, another challenge to my imagination.

I first read *Cien Años de Soledad* in English. In 1963, the Spanish version was assigned reading for my Latin American literature class, whose kind Chilean professor, Fernando Alegría, would have forgiven me if he'd known I'd read it in English. What I didn't know was that within two years I'd be living not far from Márquez's mythical town of Macondo as a Peace Corps volunteer.

The recent death of Gabriel García Márquez prompted me to read again—this time in Spanish—his epic novel, which traces the Buendía family over one hundred years. Fifty years after my posting in Colombia, García Márquez's wild, extravagant tale stirs up old memories entangled in cobwebs. Half-forgotten smells, flavors, and feelings come alive.

Barranquilla, in northern Colombia, across the Magdalena River from the province where Macondo lies, greeted me with a blast of heat, humidity, squadrons of mosquitoes, decaying buildings, and the stench of rot. The marginal barrios where I lived and worked had grown up on the periphery of the city on eroded slopes of red earth, sparsely populated with the occasional shrub and spindly tree.

My initial reaction was shock. I had always been a lover of the natural world, but how was I to love that place? The harsh extremes of climate and geography required that I make severe inner adjustments. As author Kathleen Norris said of the Dakota

26

landscape, "[T]he region requires you wrestle with it before it bestows a blessing." So I wrestled.

It took little imagination for the phantasmal tales from Macondo to remind me of the dust devils that swirled along the unpaved barrio roads in the dry season, following the multicolored buses in which I'd sit, wedged among brown bodies, lurching in counterpoint to meringue music from Caracol Radio, red fringes and saints' images swaying over the windshield. Months of heavy rains followed, renewing at night the wonderful, deafening chorus of frogs, ensconced in pools of gluey mud that clung to my shoes, while the god of thunder prepared his drums to shake my house to its foundations. Giant cockroaches, antennae waving as they crept down my bedroom walls, became the monsters of my nightmares. Maybe they were the bearers of the insomnia that afflicted the people of Macondo. For an uninterrupted night's sleep, I resorted to sleeping under a mosquito net.

My barrio neighbors were migrants to the city, rootless, as was the first generation of the Buendía family. Squatters, my neighbors erected feeble, temporary shacks that became permanent with dirt floors, wobbly furniture, bare lightbulbs overhead, walls decorated with gaudy calendars, and black-and-white daguerreotypes of solemn-faced grandparents whose bones lay buried in some country cemetery. As in Macondo, the streets had no names, locations indicated by landmarks—the street of the *palo blanco* or the ceibo tree. I felt toughened and proud that I had learned to maneuver my way through the labyrinth of winding barrio roads, even at night.

Macondo-like country customs spilled over into those barrios. Straight-backed mulattas passed by my house, balancing tin bowls on their heads, offering avocados and fragrant mangoes.

One evening I watched a group of barrio men playing their flutelike *gaitas* while the women danced the *cumbia* in a circle, their raised hands holding lit candles. The local men wore the black-and-beige straw campesino hats for protection from the searing sun. Boys on burros, laden with boxes of charcoal, sold the fuel for kitchen fires. From the doorway of my cinder-block house, I bought water from two boys driving a burro-drawn cart, loaded with large oil drums fitted with spigots. I learned to live with the bare necessities and have cherished simple living ever since.

The Buendías' battle with the mildew and *comejénes* (termites) that chewed their way through the family's furniture and walls brought back to me the stench of the mold that stained the pages of my books and the *comejénes* that carved tunnels through my shabby bedroom cabinet, scattering trails of sawdust among my clothes.

My neighbors would have fit comfortably into Márquez's novel. Many a morning, I waved over my backyard wall to Delia, gray-haired and toothless, talking loudly to herself nonstop, her complaints directed to anyone within hearing distance, as she washed clothes in an outdoor tub. It wouldn't have surprised me if one evening she'd careened off into the sky, cackling, aboard a broomstick.

Dominga, my cigar-smoking housemate and dear friend, kept me laughing even on the hardest days. Dressed in her white housecoat, closed at the top with a safety pin, she provided affection and humor that acted as my antidote to the cockroaches, the stifling humidity, and Delia's gloomy vibes. Illiterate, single mother and grandmother of five, her feet firmly planted on the earth, Dominga was my Ursula, the Buendía family matriarch. She grounded me in the coastal ways, sharing her opinions and local gossip, rife with rivalries, rumors, superstitions, *mal de ojo* (the evil eye), and mysterious *aires* (drafts). Her brown face crinkled up like a large prune, she conversed with her two parrots perched on a kitchen rafter: "*Lorito, lorito real, para la España no, sino pa'Portugal.*" (Little parrot, royal parrot, not to Spain, but to Portugal.)

All was real. The dampness, the mildew, the malnourished children, the illnesses and deaths were not products of someone's imagination. Life was precarious and fragile, yet I discovered magic in the music, the smiles, and the generosity that flourished in that inhospitable landscape.

Like a phantom from the past, I want to return—to taste fried plantains again, hear the wild chorus of nighttime frogs, and face that extreme climate and landscape that revealed to me my inner strength. Names and faces surface from the depths of memory—the blessings bestowed on me: Dominga, Ana, Anselmo, Juan, Petra. Will some remember me, or will they not know me—just as Amaranta Ursula and Aureliano Buendía failed to recognize the vagrant uncle who appeared at their door, because no one was left to tell them the old stories?

I tell my Colombia stories to anyone who will listen: my sons, Danny and Nicolás (Nico); Santiago; new and old friends; former Peace Corps colleagues. My return journey to California after I completed my Peace Corps assignment became, unexpectedly, a story worth telling.

Travels with Benjamin

Colombia, 1966. Twenty-three years old and seasoned by our two-year Peace Corps stint, we were cocky, confident, and keen on adventure. Barbara, Noel, and I decided to wend our way back to the United States via Central America and Mexico. My friends were posted together in the interior; I was on the coast. We wrote back and forth.

"I'm not sure I'm ready for the US yet."

"Me neither. I have no idea what I want to do when I get back."

"Let's just take off. We can stop to visit Faye in Costa Rica."

"I've heard Guatemala is fantastic."

Unburdened by timetables, itineraries, or reservations, we would first fly to San Andrés, a Colombian island in the Caribbean, off the coast of Nicaragua. From there we'd travel by any cheap means available. We gave no thought to political unrest, lurking guerrillas, or precarious modes of transportation. Our plan—or nonplan—had our families frantic with anxiety: three young women traveling alone through unhealthy, unsafe regions, where presidents wore military fatigues and walls bore messages of "Yanqui Go Home!" But what did parents know?

I said farewell to my Colombian friends in the barrio where I worked in Barranquilla and piled my baggage into a dilapidated taxi.

"*Al aeropuerto, por favor,*" I told the driver.

Inside the muggy, one-room building, I spotted Barbara and Noel in the milling crowd. We hugged and laughed, all three chattering at once as we lined up to check in our luggage. Then I noticed, beside Noel, a large birdcage with a live occupant.

"Meet Benjamín," said Noel.

Benjamín had every reason to be vain. The large, shiny feathers on his back, wings, and long tail shimmered a brilliant teal, and the soft, short plumes on his chest and head a bright yellow. His eyes, ringed with large white circles crossed with black stripes, gave him the air of a circus clown. His face narrowed into a long, curved beak. He was truly a fine specimen of a macaw, or *guacamayo* in local lingo.

"He's going with us?" I had difficulty envisioning the logistics.

"Where I go, Benjamín goes." Noel flashed her toothy grin.

"Does he have a passport, or whatever it is birds need?" I asked.

"Yep, got all his papers." She patted her bulging handbag.

A voice on the loudspeaker urged passengers to San Andrés to begin boarding. Through the windows we watched Benjamín in his cage, bouncing across the tarmac atop the baggage.

In spite of my misgivings, Benjamín adapted well to hotel life on San Andrés, finding the shower curtain rod a most suitable perch. For all his exotic beauty, he lacked any trace of pomposity; he was a well-educated, friendly youth. His needs were minimal: fruit, seeds, and water, and an occasional stroll outside his cage to stretch. He basked in our attention, lifting his pinions so we could tickle his wing pits and cock his head at our inept parrot talk.

We tried Spanish.

"Cara de huevo." Egg face.

He sidled back and forth on his perch but said nothing.

We tried English.

"Benjamín want a cracker?" He gurgled contentedly, a macaw version of a cat's purr, then startled us with a loud squawk. But our efforts were in vain.

After a few days of soaking up the sun on San Andrés's white sands and motorbiking around the island, we looked for transportation to the mainland. A man selling mangoes on a street corner told us that there was a boat leaving for Colón, Panama, the next day.

Captain Archibald looked doubtfully at us three, pale-skinned *gringas* and our two-foot-tall macaw but finally waved us on.

Loaded with our bags, Benjamín, and provisions for the overnight trip, we boarded the well-weathered craft. No thought of lifeboats or life jackets. As for the boat's seaworthiness . . . well, it floated and was headed in the right direction.

On board, amid the chocolate and black skin hues of the half-dozen passengers and crew, we were like curds of cottage cheese accidentally dropped into a plate of caviar. Captain Archibald assigned us to first-class quarters, two dingy cabins outfitted with small bunks and bare, stained mattresses. The others slept in the cooling breezes of the deck. In the late afternoon, as the little boat headed southwest through churning waters, we climbed the steps to the steering house to chat with the captain.

"What time will we arrive in Colón?"

"What are these instruments for?"

"What's the weather forecast?"

We gazed through the windows at the deep blue waters of the Caribbean rolling around us in a seemingly endless expanse. But as the sun waned, the mounting waves grew into liquid walls looming ominously over our small vessel. Like a cork, it rose at the mercy of the surging swells, instantly plunging into deep troughs. I had dealt with a variety of discomforts over the past two years—flying cockroaches, gooey mud clinging to my shoes, damp sheets in the rainy season and gritty sheets in the dry season—but they had all been on terra firma. The boat lurched downward yet again. I grabbed for a railing and heaved my lunch directly onto Captain Archibald's shoes.

In the morning, we went on deck to the sight of a calmed sea.

"We'll be arriving in the Colón harbor shortly," said the captain. "A US customs official will be coming onboard to check for contraband."

"Contraband?"

"You know. Fresh meat, vegetables, drugs, live animals."

We scurried to the cabin to cover Benjamín's cage with coats and implored him not to make a peep. I have since heard that women have tried smuggling parrots across borders by drugging them and stuffing them into their bras. Not even Dolly Parton could have accommodated Benjamín. Feigning innocence, we greeted the uniformed customs official and followed his every move about the boat. He opened the door to the cabin where Benjamín was ensconced. We stood silent, watching. That sound—was that a sunflower seed being cracked open? No. As if sensing what was at stake, Benjamín stayed quiet as a clam, and the coat-covered cage aroused no suspicions. We could breathe again.

But Benjamín faced another test: Panamanian customs. Captain Archibald reassured us, "It's Sunday. *Los muchachos* at customs will be hung over from last night's drinking bout. Standards'll be more relaxed."

He was right. Benjamín needed only one more official paper with the proper stamp and signature. There were street riots in Colón that day, but a determined Noel left on her errand.

Barbara and I watched the clock in our hotel room and waited. Finally, Noel returned with a grin on her face, waving the certificate triumphantly.

The next day, we took the train from Colón to Panama City along the canal. Benjamín traveled perched on the back of our seat, taking in the sights like any other tourist. As the train clickity-clacked along, curious children came to pet him and share their snacks. He drew as much attention as the ships in the canal. In Panama City, intent on exploring, we again left him on the shower rod. It was the easiest place to clean up bird droppings.

We then opted to fly via a local DC-3 propeller plane to Costa Rica. In the San José airport, a customs official examined each of Benjamín's official papers, stamped and signed in triplicate. He shook his head.

"*Lo siento*. I'm sorry, but this bird cannot enter Costa Rica."

"But he's got papers from Panama and a Colombian vet's certificate," protested Noel.

"These papers are not valid in Costa Rica." He shoved them back at her.

Perhaps if it had been a Sunday, Benjamín would have fared better. He was declared an *avis non grata* and not allowed to leave the airport. We had introduced an illegal alien into the country.

"What'll I do now?" Noel was desperate.

"The bird can fly out on the next flight to El Salvador," the officer said.

"But I don't have the money to fly to El Salvador," implored Noel. The customs man shrugged.

No way was Noel going to part with Benjamín. Her only option was to travel by bus to El Salvador while Benjamín flew.

Since Barbara and I had plans to spend some time with a friend in Costa Rica, our traveling trio would have to split.

Early the next morning, a dejected Noel stood in line at the bus station with her bags. "We can meet up at Lake Atitlán in Guatemala—or Mexico City," we said. She gave a halfhearted smile, hugged each of us, and boarded the bus for the long journey to El Salvador and her reunion with Benjamín. As the bus pulled out of the station, we saw her face peering back at us through the window and her hand waving adios.

Barbara and I traveled for the next weeks through Costa Rica, Guatemala, and Mexico. At bus and train stations, airports, plazas, and markets, we kept an eye out for Noel and Benjamín. But there was no sign of them, not a word or a squawk.

After returning to the United States, we waited for news of them. Had Noel been forced to abandon Benjamín somewhere in Central America? Or had she managed to get him across the US border and back to Louisiana, her home state? Finally, we heard through the Peace Corps grapevine that Benjamín was doing time in quarantine somewhere in Texas.

Whether Benjamín passed his final red-tape hurdle to be declared a legal US resident remains a mystery. Whenever Barbara and I visit, one of us inevitably muses, "I wonder whatever happened to Noel and Benjamín." I like to think that a determined Noel and an irresistible Benjamín, two free spirits, found happiness together on the edge of some secluded Louisiana bayou, where Benjamín could show off his plumage to the local fauna and squawk to his heart's desire—and thumb his beak at all customs officials.

II. THIS CHILEAN LIFE

Life circumstances have changed the shape and texture of my Chilean days in recent decades. Our boys left home to travel and study abroad. Soon I retired from my teaching job to have more time to pursue my writing interests and was happy to discover Santiago Writers, an English-language writing group. Retirement also allowed me more time to visit and supervise the care for my aging mother. Her death at eighty-nine, of pneumonia, felt at first like a severance of my ties with California. Yet, while dealing with my grief, I found that I had more free time and also, thanks to an inheritance she left me, greater financial independence, which opened a variety of life options for me: travel, charitable work, writing workshops, book publishing. I became a grandmother of twin girls, followed by a third girl and, most recently, a little boy, who rounded out the fullness of my days.

My Story

"*Tan linda tu historia,*" he said.

I leaned in closer to hear him over the strident, pounding racket. On the dance floor, dozens of young people jumped and shouted, flinging arms in the air.

"What story?" I asked.

"How you gave up everything—family and country—for love. To come here and live at the other end of the world. How were you able to make such a decision?" His words wafted on waves of wine-scented breath.

I doubted he'd remember our conversation the next day. How much effort did I want to invest to answer these potent questions? Besides, I was tired after sitting at this wedding banquet for more than nine hours, carrying on small talk in Spanish with the other guests at our table. Once the loud dance music started, I caught only words and phrases in the din, smiling and nodding as if in agreement with whatever was being said. Hours of that became torture.

We'd started off at noon on a bright, warm fall day for the wedding ceremony, to be held in a colonial adobe chapel in the countryside. Like most Chilean weddings, it began late. My stomach grumbled as we drove to the reception at a large country house, where several hundred guests spread out across the expansive lawns or sought shade under broad old trees. Black-aproned waiters served champagne, pineapple-basil juice, and canapés until we were summoned to a ballroom-size white tent, where we sat at our assigned table. Lunch was served at about four o'clock, along with copious amounts of fine wine, followed by a dessert buffet, where I made a weak attempt at exercising willpower.

It was still light outside when the bride and groom danced the traditional waltz. Then the DJ switched to indescribable music dictated by the tastes of the young generation, the volume raised to deafening decibels. From then on, things went downhill for me. I barely knew the others at our table. Santiago took off to join his jogging pals gathered like football players in a huddle, wineglasses in hand. I had to *do* something, so I headed to another table to chat with two women with whom I knew I could carry on a conversation beyond small talk.

It was hours later when my husband's friend perched on the chair next to me and wanted to hear "my story."

"When you voted, which country's elections excited you most?"

I pretended to hesitate. "Uh . . . the States."

"Do your boys feel more Chilean or American?"

"Chilean. After all, they were born and raised here."

"Do you regret your decision?"

Oh, boy, he was treading on dangerous territory. But I dipped into my stock of appropriate answers: my parents' heartbreak, my being their only child, and that when I married in Chile, I thought the plan was that we'd return to California. I concluded, "I have no close family left in the States. My family is here now."

He went on to sing lengthy praises of my hubby, such a fine person, an example for all, et cetera, et cetera. I smiled while looking over to the man in question for signs that we might leave soon. But he didn't see me.

This was not the only time I've felt cornered. An occasional clueless Chilean man, when discovering I'm married to one, will ask, "And how has your chileno husband turned out?" Chuckle, chuckle. They expect me to sing the praises of Chilean men, but the question does not have one simple answer.

Santiago's friend continues, "In fact, if I'd been born a woman, I would have married him myself." Bending over, he plants a warm kiss on my cheek and moves on to join the guys.

Culinary Solitary Confinement

In his article "Why Cook?," Michael Pollan discusses the undeniable trend that Americans are cooking less and buying more prepared meals, freeing housewives from kitchen slavery in order to produce in the workplace. Yet Pollan goes on to argue in favor of the shared family meal and the power of cooking to transform us from mere consumers into producers. I wholeheartedly agree—about the part regarding shared family meals. Life's circumstances altered my thoughts on cooking.

I learned to cook from my mother, and later, living on my own in Berkeley, I expanded my culinary skills to include recipes from Mexican friends. When I arrived in Chile, Mexican was not an option, and a severe food shortage posed great challenges for cooks. I found here most of the same fruits and vegetables as in California, their climates being so similar. Short on meatless recipes, I bought a small cookbook of simple, traditional Chilean dishes. I'd make tuna-and-Swiss-chard casseroles, shepherd's pie, and fish croquettes. My mother-in-law explained how to soak dogfish shark in milk to eliminate the ammonia odor and gave me her recipe for lemon pudding. However, I soon discovered that most people have maids do their cooking. At first, we hired a daily maid, but after the birth of Nico, our second son, I reluctantly gave in to Santiago's pressure to hire a live-in maid. I did the grocery shopping and planned the meals, but the maid did the major cooking. I returned to full-time teaching, happy to have help in the kitchen.

By the time I retired, I'd lost interest in cooking, or, to be honest, I'd become lazy, accustomed to having Carola, our sweet-tempered, part-time maid, do it for me. I plan meals, shop, give her recipes to follow, and sometimes work side by side with her. Although I enjoy typical Chilean dishes, like empanadas and *pastel de choclo* (corn pie), I don't have the motivation to take on their time-consuming preparation. But friends and family here claim that I make great salads, especially basic tossed salad and dressing, a skill I learned from my mother. At Christmas they know I'll be preparing my grandmother's recipe of Scottish shortbread. When I go to the Jumbo, my local supermarket, I notice newly introduced foods, like kale, gluten-free products, and Mexican salsas. I'm a strong believer in buying local, but in the middle of winter, the scent of imported California peaches in the store breaks my resolve. And nowadays, if I think we're getting into a food rut, I go to the Internet for inspiration.

Besides cooking, multiple other activities vie for my time: gardening, reading, writing, anything that frees me from kitchen isolation. Because that's one factor Michael Pollan didn't take into consideration: the size of the kitchen and its location in the house plan. Chilean kitchens were not designed as places of social gathering. Even in new, modern apartments, they are the size of a closet and separated from the other living areas by doors (because originally they were the exclusive domain of maids). The kitchen in our fifty-year-old house is long and narrow, though the addition of a small breakfast nook by the previous owners makes it more inviting. But it has doors that cut me off from the activity in the rest of the house when I'm doing last-minute preparations and serving meals. After our boys left home, the kitchen became an even lonelier place. My husband has zero interest in cooking and descends from his second-floor office only when I call out, "Dinner's ready!"

As the supply of women willing to work as maids declines,

cocinas americanas, American kitchens, meaning a kitchen incorporated into a sitting or dining room, are now a big selling point for many new homes here. I've fantasized about taking a sledgehammer to the wall separating my kitchen from our den, but it would create a gigantic mess and leave me with considerably less storage space.

The kitchen in my childhood home had a sunny breakfast nook, and when my parents remodeled the kitchen, they exchanged the swinging door leading to the dining room for a sliding one that usually stayed open. While washing the dishes, we faced a large window that looked out onto a grand old oak.

For the past thirty years in our Santiago home, the wall of our next-door neighbor's house has been my kitchen-sink view.

No wonder I'd rather be in the garden.

The Morning with Oscar

The frost is still sparkling on the ground and rooftops as Oscar, our occasional gardener, pulls up in his 1992 beige Volkswagen van. I hear the van chugging to a stop, and I sigh with relief. He's arrived. I say "occasional" because he is a no-show more often than not, which is not unusual here in Chile, where gardeners tend to be as unpredictable as spring weather. I put up with his unreliable ways because I like him. He and I are botanical soul mates.

Growing up on a quarter acre of California hillside in the presence of two gardener parents, I developed early on a knowledge of and love for plants and soil. I helped, cutting dead roses or watering potted geraniums. Most of the same fruits and vegetables, flowers and trees grow here as in California. I just had to learn their Spanish names. Only after settling in Chile, where we bought our first house, did I have a garden of my own.

Clad in baggy khaki pants, blue flannel shirt, and baseball cap, Oscar slides open the van's side door. He's brought me a present, *un regalo*, he says, pulling out a rectangular plastic flower pot planted with a variety of herbs: mint, cilantro, thyme, oregano, dwarf celery.

Surprised and pleased, I thank him, though I suspect it's his way of apologizing for his absences.

Today we need to prune the bougainvillea, I tell him, and the lemon tree needs shaping. We discuss which branches are to be pruned to allow more sunlight to play through.

Problems kept him away, he says, poking at the dichondra, declaring it's looking good. Just wait till spring, he says. The garden will be beautiful. He clops about in his thick work boots, leaving a trail of mud clods on the patio. Oscar put this garden in for me last spring and takes an interest in how everything is faring. Planning and planting it was our mutual labor of love.

High up on the ladder, he wrestles with the thorny bougainvillea, snips away, and tosses the branches down to the ground, and we chat. I ask him about insect-repelling plants and ones that will attract ladybugs. I'd like to put in some forget-me-nots and baby violets, I tell him. He offers to bring me some two-toned primulas. He runs a small nursery and brings me plants he knows I'll like—the California poppies he put in the front yard and the black-eyed Susans trailing on the back wall. I bring him coffee (three teaspoons of sugar) and wire to tie up bundles of branches.

Oscar is not a big man, but he's strong and fit. He breaks up the branches with his rough hands, dirt caked underneath his fingernails. I ask him why he doesn't wear gloves. He works better with his bare hands, he says. As a no-gloves gardener myself, I empathize with him. My sense of touch guides me to work the tender roots into the soil.

"Oscar, *por favor*, if something comes up and you can't make it, call me."

"*Sí, señora*," he says. "I'll be back in fifteen days."

He lurches off in the van, and I look about my garden with satisfaction. He has waved his magic wand and coaxed the beauty out from under winter's ravages. Soon spring will tiptoe in to round out Oscar's magic.

Green Salad Bowl

In the first days of spring, I felt the urge for bright colors. A green salad bowl in our local store caught my eye. We'd been in a salad-bowl rut, using the same scratched, clear plastic one with the yellow rim for years. Definitely time for a change.

The new bowl demanded new place mats. The edges of our old brown ones bore puppy nibbles from our beagle, Max, who'd died ten years earlier. After considerable searching, I found the perfect cheery green placemats. And how could I not buy the matching designer napkins? Green glasses and votive candle holders added the final touch.

Spring is nature's time of renewal, so why not introduce a few changes into my kitchen to lift my winter-weary spirit?

But this consumerist bent of mine troubles me. A confirmed believer in traveling lightly through this life, I detest accumulating clutter and enjoy organizing closets and throwing things out. Trips to the recycling center are tremendously satisfying. When I turned sixty, I decided I had all the necessary baggage. No need to purchase more for the house. *This will be the last washing machine I'll ever have to buy.* How creeping old age changes my idea of what constitutes necessities.

At my favorite kitchen store, I held a battery-run beater for frothing milk for cappuccinos and asked myself, *Do I really need this? Will it fit into my already overcrowded utensil drawer? Can my money be spent in a better way?* Only if an object passes the test do I give myself permission to purchase it. I didn't buy the beater—then.

So far, my acquisitive urge has stopped at the kitchen door. That's not counting the new rosebush I just bought, or the enormous blue ceramic pot that houses it. Painting the inside of the house this month isn't materialistic, is it? That's not actually *buying* something. But the fresh paint may require new curtains. The rain-stained ones in the living and dining rooms have lasted over twenty years. "Who notices the stains?" my husband asks. I do.

Once the walls are painted, the fading of the striped upholstery on the living room chairs will be more noticeable. And that ugly upholstery on the sofa bed in the study—it'll need something lighter. Not green, but brighter.

I tell myself that renovating and improving aren't necessarily the antithesis of "light traveling." What motivates me, I wonder—the desire to create beauty in my surroundings? I'm a perfectionist, like my mother, and can't resist mentally "fixing up" the abandoned park or the dark, vine-covered house on the corner. Spring fever? It could be a physical condition, as its name implies.

But maybe it's about control, too. There's nothing I can do about my batwing arms and turkey neck, worsening vision, or unreliable memory. But a face-lift for my house and garden— these I can still do something about. They do wonders for my spirit. Why should it flag just because my body is?

A visiting niece exclaims, "I love coming to this house!" Beauty brings pleasure not only to me, but to family and friends. The green salad bowl and all that followed are my gift to them. So I tell myself.

Bicentennial Mutt

The dog bore all the signs of a stray: no collar, mottled white fur with black patches. The perfect stand-in for Harry the Dirty Dog. Of no identifiable breed, he wore a tail that looked as though it had been caught in several fast-closing doors. Trotting along in the park in my direction, he seemed to have a clear destination in mind. I made a couple of kissing noises. He stopped. At my "Hi, doggie," he wagged his crooked tail and looked at me with dark eyes. Love at first sight. I walked on, and he followed me. Now I was in trouble. His plight saddened me, but I didn't want another dog. Twelve years of Max, our untrainable beagle, was enough. But I can't resist talking to the ubiquitous strays populating the streets of my adopted city.

A few days later, when I spotted a newspaper photograph of a street dog being escorted outside a barricade by a stern *carabinero*, I was curious. The dog looked humiliated. *Such indignity.* The grounds of La Moneda, the presidential palace, were being readied for a ceremony, and mutts were not invited. Yet the occasion was honoring one of its kind. As part of Chile's bicentennial celebration, president Michelle Bachelet would be honoring the winners of a photography competition, "The Bicentennial Street Dog."

They deserve the honor. The stray mongrels are emblematic of this country. They wander into soccer games and onto the red carpet rolled out from the presidential palace for visiting dignitaries. They instinctively gravitate to construction sites, where the workers adopt them as pets, christen them with names like Cachupín and Washington, and feed them portions of their lunches. Favoring the busy streets downtown, the dogs sleep in doorways, against walls, or in the middle of the sidewalk. The street vendors take pity on the "regulars," sharing rations with them. One afternoon, I saw four mutts dozing in the shade of a coastal bus stop under a tsunami evacuation sign. Oh, to have had my camera.

It doesn't matter if they're unwashed, battle-scarred, short-legged, or dreadlocked—they're street-savvy survivors, hungry for companionship. Perhaps that's why Chileans tolerate and even defend the strays. In some way, they can identify with them. Maybe the homeless canines remind them of the *roto chileno*. This collective hero has his origins in the young campesino who was recruited, with no training or uniform, to fight in the war of 1839 against Peru and Bolivia and is known for his audacity and bravery. Now the term is used often in a derogatory manner, referring to the down-and-out, the uneducated, the low-class laborer. But those considered in that category are proud to call themselves *rotos*. Like the strays, they're resilient and loyal.

Periodically, the problem of the abundant strays becomes a hot issue, the subject of television reports and letters to newspaper editors. Recently, dozens of abandoned dogs on a rural road outside the city caused a furor. Residents from a nearby town were feeding the dogs. Others contended that they should be removed, but the dog lovers yelped in protest. Since the town lacked the resources to care for or neuter them, the strays could come to a sad end. Not long ago, I traveled down that road, and the scene of the strays soliciting like beggars along the road's edge is one I can't forget. Sadly, as long as there's poverty and an inadequate sense of responsible pet ownership, I think the strays are here to stay.

This poses a moral dilemma for me. They are hungry and homeless and dirty. Shouldn't I contact an organization for rescue dogs? How can I do nothing? The truth is, I don't want to take on the responsibility. I feel a stab of guilt. This is not the attitude of a Good Samaritan, although if I find a dog with a tag, I do call the owner and wait until he arrives. Every week, the trees and posts in the park where I walk are papered with fresh computer-printed ads for lost dogs, bearing a tender photo of the canine in question and offering a reward. I'm sad for the owner and the pooch and wish them a happy reunion.

Now our local park offers me a more positive canine scene: pups of all sizes and breeds romping and chasing in newly installed dog parks. I sit on a bench and watch their comic cavorting. Their gaiety is contagious. I pray that this civic concern spreads to the less fortunate neighborhoods, where strays continue to wander in need of tender loving care.

Table Talk

One of Santiago's cyclist friends invites us to a barbecue. After several hours, the meat is finally ready and the men have exhausted the topic of cycling. Seated at the long table, I try to follow the different strains of lively conversation. In spite of the decades I've lived here, I tend to be quiet at large social gatherings, self-conscious of my accented Spanish. This allows me to listen and observe and learn—especially when it comes to politics.

Even four decades after the military coup, the circumstances preceding and following it remain a frequent, sensitive subject of differing and strong opinions. Tonight is no exception, as the conversation turns to Chile's painful past during the Allende government and the military government that followed, now often referred to as the military dictatorship. (Interesting how one word changes the perception.) Tonight I sense an increased openness, or maybe a softening of the rigid stance of those on the pro-Pinochet political Right, which comprises most of the guests present. Everyone listens as one guest gives what I think to be a balanced evaluation of the military government, summing up the good (the establishment of a successful economic program) and the bad (tragic human rights violations). I'm surprised that no one disputes his points. Have they moved slightly out of their bastions of denial?

I arrived in Chile a year before the coup, so I experienced a "before" and an "after," as well as the return to democracy. What I did not experience and what must be factored into any understanding of the past is Chile's political and social history prior to Allende. With the perspective of hindsight, those at the table have access to a more comprehensive view of their nation's recent history, which has made me reluctant to voice my political opinions. Do I have the right? I take very seriously my right to vote. Though my understanding of Chile's history is superficial, as an expat voter I possess the unique advantage of having no ties to any political party—a benefit that allows me to have a more open mind. A presidential election is fast approaching. I'm listening to what the candidates have to say, while most Chileans stay stuck with their original party allegiances.

Those here tonight are concerned about the socialist direction of the present government, fearing a return to the past. Much of the population is too young to have that advantage of perspective, while others seem to have forgotten or are easily swayed by clever slogans. Others have pain and anger so deep that they cannot forgive.

I have been an observer of Chileans' ongoing struggle to reconcile their differences, to forgive and ask for forgiveness. Recent Chilean history has opened a window of awareness to me. I now can appreciate the complexity of the painful reconciliation process, a process that nations, ethnicities, and minorities throughout history have undergone and currently experience wherever violence and war are waged.

I'm reminded of the lyrics to Bob Dylan's "Blowin' in the Wind," which we used to sing in the 1960s during the Vietnam War. My generation was idealistic and believed peace was possible. We joined the Peace Corps by the thousands. Little would we have imagined that the lyrics of the song would be just as relevant fifty or sixty years into the future. Now older, perhaps wiser, we understand the messiness of war and conflict, that there is no clear black and white. Despite the current state of events worldwide, I continue to cling to hope, remembering how we'd sing about giving peace a chance.

III. MY ADOPTED COUNTRY

Chile in the year of my arrival, 1972, was immersed in social, economic, and political turmoil, beleaguered by protest marches, strikes, and shortages of food and basic necessities. A year later, a military coup ousted president Salvador Allende, and for the next eighteen years we lived under a military dictatorship. Adjusting to the novelty of another country, making do with shortages, and holding a full-time teaching job kept me occupied. Standing in line at the supermarket to buy a chicken didn't leave space to think about missing the family, friends, and places I'd left behind. It wasn't until later that I realized how privileged I'd been to have grown up in that small town surrounded by rolling hills and rich vegetation. Living in this city, situated amid dry hills populated by cactus and no nearby forests, I missed the scents of the golden California hillside grass, of redwood and bay trees. My close-up view of the majestic Andes mountains from my window here has been my consolation. I wrote in my journal, "Perhaps I had to travel the road that I did in order to realize that earth, grass, mountain, and sky are my sustenance." Developing familiarity with this land of crazy geography, immersing myself in its rich, varied landscapes, is the path I found to deal with my sense of loss.

Perspective

Last night I dreamed of mountains. This comes as no surprise, given that I've crossed the Andes (Cordillera to locals) by land twice in the past three days. Living in Santiago, I have always used them as a point of reference for my internal compass. The sun rises from behind those looming rocky ridges and illuminates them as it sets. I know that if I'm heading toward the mountains, I'm going east. I can always count on the peak of El Plomo to be there, even when it's hidden by a veil of smog.

Heading to Mendoza in Argentina's wine country, where Santiago would run a half-marathon, we followed the rising, winding road carved from rock—along ledges, through tunnels, bordering rivers—into the heart of the Cordillera. The surrounding peaks, cliffs, and canyons closed in, swallowing us in their wild terrain. Midway through the Cristo Redentor tunnel, we passed from Chile to Argentina. Emerging from the tunnel, we descended into a landscape of pale green slopes and alpine valleys. To our left, the snow of Mt. Aconcagua, the highest in the western and southern hemispheres, at 22,837 feet, shimmered in splendor, contrasting with a deep-blue sky. I search for words to describe how the sight made me feel: euphoric, in awe, blessed. Later, we passed a small hill enclosed by a low rock wall, the burial grounds for climbers defeated by Aconcagua.

As we descended onto the flat, vast Argentine plains, the vegetation changed to tufts of long grass, long, waving foxtails, and scrubby bushes, interspersed with neat vineyards. My perspective of the land changed as well. Now the sun would set behind the Andes, and I knew that far into the east lay the Atlantic. Rather than El Plomo, my view encompassed Aconcagua and the Tupungato volcano, new points of reference for three days.

To develop an inner sense of place on the eastern side of the Cordillera would have required more time. Sense of place wants more than compass reference points. For "place" bonds to form, I need familiarity with the birdsong, the scents of vegetation, the names of the trees, and the lay of the land, and if I interact with that place, it evokes strong, valued memories.

Returning home, we headed west, back up into those ridges, and then descended the *caracol*, the mountainside of twenty-nine switchbacks (which, the customs officer gleefully informed us, was one of the world's ten most dangerous roads), into Chile. I felt welcomed by the familiar rock formations and peaks that ground me on this land, where the sun rises from behind the peaks and sets over the Pacific.

Weeds

The gardener came Wednesday, and in a few hours he had it looking tidier, dead flowers and scraggly shoots cut, bushes trimmed, backyard grass mowed. I always gently suggest that he pull a few weeds, but caution is necessary, because I've learned that Chilean gardeners do not consider weeding part of their job. One previous gardener, Nelson, whose quick sense of humor always had me chuckling, resigned, saying, "Your garden has too many weeds."

This created a dilemma for me, since my body no longer takes to the postures weeding requires. I've had to make some concessions in this battle, ceding victory to the determined oxalis that has invaded the lawn in the backyard with its labyrinthine root system. At least it's green and bears perky yellow flowers. I do pull the leafier weeds that have shallow, single roots. I have a handy tool for the purpose.

Michael Pollan wrote a whole chapter on weeds in his book *Second Nature.* I reread his "Weeds are Us" chapter this morning, hoping to stimulate my creative juices, but realized it would be presumptuous of me to think I have anything to add to such entertaining prose. I can refer only to my own garden experiences.

I've been aiming for the appearance of a wild garden—no manicured looks for me—gradually introducing Chilean native plants alongside a few California natives (do not inquire how they got here). Here is our oasis, for beyond the city limits the landscape has turned brown, arid, and dusty. More grass fires have added ash to the mix. The forestry service reports an 800 percent increase in land burned, compared with last year. How fragile is our earth, and we along with it.

I've learned that if I want a "wild garden," it doesn't pay to be hasty. What may at first resemble a weed could be a welcome "volunteer," deposited here by a visiting austral thrush or a sparrow. Allow the seedling time, and I may be in for a surprise. Our garden surprises include sunny black-eyed Susans and a jacaranda tree that explodes into purple blooms in the spring. I'm looking forward to discovering the identity of two newcomers that seem to be developing into handsome shrubs. As with all things plant-related, I must wait and watch.

Wind

Wind is a wily character, always stirring things up, moving things around, never content to let things just *be*.

Thank goodness.

Right now it's having great fun tossing yellowing leaves off their perches and chasing them along the ground. The branches of even the most stiff and formal trees succumb to the wind's force. Leaves flutter on branches, waving like a chorus of children's hands. Trickster wind, always changing, making clouds look like shredded cotton batting. And beware, you prickly conifers. The wind loves to peek under your wide, full skirts.

It takes special delight in messing up my hair, but if I forget my appearance, I relish the feel of the wind on my face. Colorless, transparent, intangible, yet an instigator, a messenger, reshaping sand dunes, sculpting rocks, deforming trees, carrying seeds and the smell of frying onions from my neighbor's house, or more welcome fragrances of wet leaves, pine needles, the salty sea.

Away from city noises, I notice the sounds of the wind: soughing through pine branches, howling around the eaves of the house, whistling through electric wires.

When I was a child, I'd lie in my bed, listening to the tapping of rain and the swishing of tree branches outside my window. My contentment lay in the contrast of my snug bed with the wild goings-on outside. City wind here lacks the drama of the Pacific Coast storms that buffeted my hometown. These days, my winter contentment lies in a good book, a comfortable chair by the radiator, and a window view of the workings of the wind. Wind has many names: gale, breeze, puff, blast, draft, gust. And many skills: it propels sailboats and windmills, whips flags on their poles, spins the weather vane and the wings on my whirligig duck. This morning I stepped outside to a shaggy carpet of gold and burgundy liquidambar leaves on the sidewalk. The trickster had paid us a visit in the night.

Dry Days

I've learned that grass smells great and wind feels amazing and rain is a miracle. —Astronaut Scott Kelly

A line of water trickles along the gutter of our sidewalk. I follow it down the street, but I can't identify its source. I do this often when out on my walks, this sleuthing to identify which neighbor is wasting water: washing his car on the street with the hose running; watering gardens midday or ignoring malfunctioning sprinklers; hosing off a driveway and sidewalk, rather than sweeping. I don't want to earn the reputation of a busybody with too much time on her hands, so I don't say, "Do you realize that Chile is in its fifth year of drought? Shouldn't we be conserving water?"

Few city dwellers consider where our water comes from. We're too far from its source. Captured from reservoirs of glacial melt high in the Andes, it's channeled into wide underground tubes and piped to buildings and homes and gardens and golf courses and fountains and pools. Turn on the faucet, and out it pours. Or pop a few bottles of water into your shopping cart. So easy. Here in Santiago, most people know it comes from the Maipo River. Fewer think about the dwindling snowmelt that feeds the rivers. Small-town residents and farmers are more aware of their dependence upon wells and shrinking reservoirs.

California, like Chile, has suffered through years of drought. In my hometown, north of San Francisco, drought awareness is high. Public bathrooms display signs reminding the public to conserve water. The low level in water district reservoirs is clearly visible to the frequent hikers and bikers. The severity of drought makes an impact when you can *see* it. I once traveled with Santiago in the fall to Yosemite National Park, for his first visit there. Not a drop of water in Yosemite Falls. I had to describe to him what the valley looked like in a normal year.

My childhood camping vacations in the Sierra always involved walks to Indian Springs to fill our canvas water bag. There was no sign indicating the way along the faint trail that passed through a meadow bright with alpine flowers and fragrant with the aroma of wild onions. Up a short slope, those of us in the know could locate the old pipe, through which poured sweet, cool, crystalline water. I want my grandchildren and every child to have the experience of *seeing* where water comes from and *hearing* the rhythmic tapping of rain on the roof.

After almost a year aboard the International Space Station, Scott Kelly commented, "I'll never take water for granted again."

The Other Extreme

Mud. And more mud. That's the scenario that the city's inhabitants will wake to tomorrow. Though it's stopped raining for the moment, after forty-eight hours of relentless downpour, the meteorologists predict the rain will continue through the night and the next day.

The Mapocho River wanted to follow its true course, its ancient, familiar bed of rock and gravel and sediment. But major works of engineering placed obstacles in its way—tunnels, holes, temporary retaining walls, subterranean underpasses—to facilitate the movement of masses of motorists rushing to destinations throughout the city. After all, we all fume when stuck in the ever-increasing traffic jams, grouching, *Why don't they do something?*

Roaring down the slopes of the Andes, gathering force and speed, the river waters suddenly confronted foreign obstacles in their path. Rivers are not patient with obstructions. They stubbornly forge onward. When its natural flow is blocked, what does the river do? It detours through the paths of least resistance: underground parking garages, subterranean malls, underpasses, basements, cracks, crevasses, mouse holes, potholes, perforations, and fissures. Because forward it will go, downhill, seaward, obeying the laws of physics.

As the water surges down drought-ridden slopes, it sucks up loose soil, rocks, and assorted plastic bottles, depositing them in the flatter areas. A recipe for a muddy mess. Though the water moves on, like an undisciplined child, it doesn't clean up what it dropped along its wild way.

Thus, out roar man's machines—pumps, bulldozers, hoses,

and trucks—to undo what nature has done. With furious urgency, they'll reestablish the obstacles and barriers, move earth, pump water, drill holes, erect stronger retention walls, widen the riverbed.

Not for the first time. Repeated interventions of the river have paralleled the growth of the city of Santiago, immediate gain being the top priority. Walls, buildings, houses, stores, and highways line the banks of the manhandled river.

There's no one around now who remembers it when it flowed freely along its natural course. I grieve for the river, for its fields and valleys, once a bucolic landscape, as portrayed by artists in the early days of settlement, and now a rushing torrent of mud soup.

Tough Lessons

Perspiration streams down my back. The air is ash-laden; another day of record-breaking high temperatures smothers and oppresses. Is this what an apocalypse feels like? An apocalypse of global warming.

In my garden, honey- and bumblebees dart about, alighting on the lacy, fragrant flowers of my *ilán-ilán* tree, their favorite right now. I wonder if this heavy air interferes with their orientation and sensitive sense of smell.

The televised scenes of forests and fields, farm animals and homes being devoured by raging flames feel unreal, more like a Hollywood disaster movie—pine trees converted into flaming torches, unidentifiable carcasses littered on the ground. A farmwoman laments her losses. "Everything," she cries. "Everything." Behind her, a scorched washing machine perches atop a pile of rubble. Veterinarians treat the wounds of a horse with a singed forelock. Beekeepers point to their blackened hives and scorched fields.

Firemen, forest rangers, soldiers, and townspeople work together to control the flames with hoses, shovels, rakes, and chain saws. Those without tools attempt to smother flames with leafy tree branches.

Relief is on the way. The 747 Global SuperTanker, thanks to a single donor's generosity, roars low over the heads of cheering country people, releasing its cargo of water and repellant onto the flaming forest. It's the star of each night's newscasts. To my surprise, I notice painted on its fuselage the words SPIRIT OF JOHN MUIR, after the naturalist, explorer, Sierra Club founder, and promoter of California's Yosemite Valley as the first US National Park.

I feel a renewed faith in humankind as I watch scenes of hundreds of cars and trucks lining up to take aid to the people of Santa Olga, a town left in ashes. Television and newspaper advertisements provide information for making monetary donations. Beekeepers beg for bags of sugar to make a solution to keep the bees from starving while their owners search for safe areas.

My garden bees, like all of their species, are well experienced in cooperation, each performing its assigned task for the benefit of the whole hive. Those foragers pollinating our apricot- and avocado-tree blossoms guarantee our summer harvest. They will return to their hives with their pollen-laden baskets, dance their waggle dance, or wave their antennae to inform the others where to find the sweet stuff. I wonder where they've established their hives in this city neighborhood. I'm amazed to learn that in winter they instinctively know to crowd together tightly, each bee rotating through the cluster from outside to inside so no bee gets too cold. In hot weather, they fan their wings. Such efficiency. No carbon footprint.

Yet, against wind-whipped wildfires, bees have little defense. They depend upon our care, which we must recognize as a mutually beneficial arrangement. Chilean beekeepers look to move their healthy hives to new lands temporarily, and I wonder how long it will take for the native foliage to recover. One year? Two? Ten? Already a winter of little rain is predicted.

Danger exists that complacency will set in now that the crisis is past. It is easy to forget lessons learned, as television and newspaper headlines devote more space to political frauds and the day's robberies. Yet the homeless are still homeless, the farmers have no suitable soil to farm, and the bees no fields and trees to visit. When will they return to their buzzing, bumbling, pollinating, and dancing the waggle, as only honeybees know how to do?

This morning, I look up to the wonder of an almost-true-blue firmament. Lightness fills me after the weeks of oppressive, smoke-filled sky. My bees dance about the delicate blooms of the *ilán-ilán*. Purposeful, passionate pollinators.

IV. IN PATAGONIA

A gigantic bronze statue of a patagón, or Tehelche native, reigns over the main plaza of the southern city of Punta Arenas. Magellan called the native people patagón, bigfoot, because they seemed giants to the smaller Europeans. The local legend claims that if you touch the burnished foot of the patagón, you will return to Patagonia. Each time I go, I make sure to honor that tradition.

In the Land of Lilliput

With a groaning and a clattering and a toot of its whistle, the ferry pulled into the landing at Caleta Gonzalo. I unfolded my map and scanned the long, thin form of Chile until I spotted our location, halfway between the 41st and 42nd parallels. Here, the country breaks up into an intricate jigsaw pattern of gulfs, fjords, and inlets with names like Salvation Bay and Gulf of Sorrows, and of islands and capes called Desolation, Hope, Refuge Point. Now, before us spreads Pumalín Park, a private ecological reserve of old-growth temperate rain forests and site of one of the few remaining stands of the endangered *alerce* trees.

Cars, backpackers, and cyclists poured off the ferry, some heading for the campground, others, like us, making their way to the cabins. Under a night sky awash with stars, we spotted a shingled structure built on wooden pillars. A chorus of frogs and the burble of water flowing beneath the cabin were the only sounds.

The next day's morning light revealed the deep green waters of the fjord, the silky surface broken occasionally by the arching bodies of a pair of dolphins. We followed a carved wooden sign indicating a trail leading into the shadows of ancient forests enclosing a narrow valley. After only a short walk along the trail, it seemed as though we had stepped into an enchanted kingdom where elves and fairies dwelled. The path on either side was dense with native saplings, bamboo, and ferns, taller than I. Lording over the undergrowth rose the tallest specimens of native trees I had ever seen: conifers, beech, laurel, myrtle, with mossy chests and sprouting armpits. Aerial plants and mosses clung to every possible surface and crevice of the trees. Upturned roots and fallen trunks housed a damp, Lilli-putian world of mosses, creepers, fungi, and lichens. Tangles of smooth, serpent-like tree roots crisscrossed the trail.

The forest dripped with moisture and echoed with the gur-gle of streams, bordered by wild fuchsias and ferns, laced with sparkling spiderwebs. We traversed boardwalks through bogs, resounding with undetectable frogs. We clambered up and down slippery log ladders on the more treacherous inclines. Fallen trees stood in as bridges, challenging my balance.

Younger hikers passed us by, intent on reaching their des-tination. We marched to our own tune, for the getting there was surely as captivating as the waterfalls at the trail's end. A sudden, loud *caw-caw* and a repeated pecking from high above stopped us in our tracks, alerting our bird-watchers' antennae. If we had possessed tails, they would have been pointing. Whip-ping out binoculars and scanning surrounding tree trunks, we got our first live view of a pair of giant Magellanic woodpeck-ers, now on Chile's Red List of endangered species. The male's bright, punk-red head and crest were breathtaking. Reluctantly, we continued on but were again sidetracked, this time by the startling, ventriloquist warble of the elusive *chucao* bird, per-haps the most characteristic sound of southern Chilean forests. Because of its rufous coloring and its preference for skulking in the shadows of the forest floor, the *chucao* is difficult to spot. Waiting motionless, we were soon rewarded for our patience. A *chucao* scurried onto our path and then stopped to poke at leaves by our feet. Finches twittered among bamboo branches and giant, tough *nalca,* or coltsfoot, leaves, which looked like snacks for dinosaurs. The abundant fuchsia flowers catered to hummingbird appetites. I was struck by the innocence and trust of the birds in those protected lands. On a boulder in the river, a southern ringed kingfisher posed for us, interrupting the preening of his chestnut, blue-gray, and white feathers for an occasional dart into the water.

Then, before us, a stand of *alerce*, or Patagonian cypress, some of the oldest and largest trees in the world, unique to the temperate rain forests of southern Chile and Argentina. Those craggy giants allowed me a deepened perspective of history; they were already one thousand years old when Spanish explorers first landed on nearby shores. High up the sinewy trunks, crooked, moss-covered branches reached skyward, as if poised in prayer. They demanded respect. I understood why in the past the now-extinct indigenous peoples venerated these survivors. They called the *alerce* tree *lahuan* (grandfather).

Access to the waterfall at the end of the trail presented the toughest physical challenge yet—pulling ourselves up blocks of rock by a rope and then ascending a ladder propped against a giant boulder. Only by reaching the top was a view of the falls possible. Drawing on my inner adventurer resources, I made the ascent (and have the photos to prove it).

On our return, treading the forest floor, spongy with rotting leaves and pungent humus, a sense of primeval forces at work came over me, an awareness of my own insignificance amid such grandeur and antiquity. Pumalín sparked in me a glimmer of hope for the future of the earth's ancient forests. I possessed a palpable vision of what was at stake, now that one of those forests was a personal acquaintance of mine.

In the Wakes of Magellan and Darwin

Our first night out to sea, standing on the deck, I felt the presence of Ferdinand Magellan. Sturdy hands on the railing of his ship *Trinidad*, the explorer may have seen this same full moon illuminate his path on the water as he searched for a route to the Pacific through this uncharted maze of islands and fjords. I'd recently read *Over the Edge of the World*, Laurence Bergreen's account of the Magellan expedition's circumnavigation of the globe from 1519 to 1522. Now I was aboard the *Vía Australis*, navigating the straits named for him. Like his flotilla, we were alone, no other ships in sight, no lights blinking from the shore, only the looming humps of dark mountains.

Embarking in blustery Punta Arenas, Chile, we cruised through the Patagonian fjords, a veritable labyrinth of capes and channels and inlets, islands and ridges, sculpted by ancient glaciers. I've traveled often to continental Patagonia, an untamed landscape of cathedral-spire peaks, emerald lakes, and endless pampas, but this time I had an ocean view. This southernmost region of South America, referred to as the "bottom of the world," spoke to me of daring climbs and dangerous expeditions.

Though just a simple tourist, I wanted to know the heart-stopping wonder and the thrill experienced by those who first navigated these southern seascapes. Anticipating the desire to keep a record of the region's startling surroundings, I packed in my suitcase a fresh, clean diary.

Why keep a travel journal? John Adams wrote to his grandsons that without a diary their travels would be "no better than a flight of birds through the air," leaving no trace. In a journal, we can go beyond the visual to find words that suggest the tingle of the salty air, the force and chill of the wind, the creaking of a glacier, the silence and solitude, and our responses to these sensual experiences.

I also brought along a small book of accounts of early travelers to these extreme latitudes. Those first visitors to this region felt compelled to chronicle their travels. Magellan contracted Italian Antonio Pigafetta to document his personal perceptions, as well as the facts of the voyage. What drew those explorers here? What hardships did they endure? Some embarked on this journey seeking to open new frontiers. Perhaps for the ordinary seaman, it was just a job. What draws us in the twenty-first century to visit rugged, distant places? Is it an urge for adventure in these times when few unexplored frontiers remain on this planet? In the safety of a modern cruise ship, we faced no likely dangers, yet I think most passengers on this ship, in the presence of a rumbling, giant glacier, couldn't help but imagine themselves as explorers. I also believe we yearn to witness the mind-boggling beauty of this endangered landscape while it's still possible.

Stories, diaries, and legends of the southernmost seas abound: of navigators like Magellan and Sir Francis Drake, and later explorers like Italian missionary Alberto de Agostini and Antarctic adventurer Ernest Shackleton. Their testimonies inspired Samuel Taylor Coleridge to write "The Rime of the Ancient Mariner":

> *The ice was here, the ice was there,*
> *The ice was all around:*
> *It cracked and growled, and roared and howled,*
> *Like noises in a swound!*

The morning of our first land excursion at Tierra del Fuego's Ainsworth Bay was bright and fresh. It was fall in the Southern Hemisphere, the April sun igniting the burnt-orange and crimson leaves of the beech trees. It was the kind of day for which Magellan and his crew must have given thanks, free from the williwaws—the great storms blowing off the glaciers. Pigafetta wrote, "I believe there is not a more beautiful or better strait than this one."

Following our guide, we stepped gently through a marsh of coarse, frost-covered grasses and shrubs bearing red berries, where meltwater from the Marinelli Glacier mingled with the sea. On the beach, we walked over wafer-thin rocks, vestiges of the passing of the glacier that had retreated ten kilometers up the valley in the past fifty years. Above, two condors soared, while a massive sea elephant lounged on a nearby sandbar.

After lunch, the ship turned into Pia Fjord, its hull crunching against chunks of ice. Delicate veils of water cascaded down the fern-covered cliffs of the milky-green fjord. The Pia Glacier came into view, its depths glimmering a pale turquoise. We boarded zodiacs, disembarked on a rocky peninsula, and climbed to a spot overlooking the glacier. The mass of ice creaked and groaned as it shifted on its granite bed, and, suddenly, a giant pillar calved and collapsed into the water with a thundering roar. Crystal flakes showered over us. How terrified Magellan's sailors must have been upon hearing those booming echoes, facing those ice walls for the first time.

I felt no fear, only childlike wonder. Magellan and his men exposed themselves to life-threatening risks in order to conquer this newfound territory for their homelands. But this was no longer an unexplored frontier, and we had come not to subjugate nature but to appreciate and learn to live in harmony with this unique, fragile landscape. Every passenger or tourist responds in a unique way to what is before her. As a simple observer, I opened my senses to allow this place to seep into my pores—the sharp air and the silence pierced by roaring glaciers—and leave its mark on me. This kind of experience influences how we each tread this earth. As writer Eudora Welty said, "One place understood helps us know all places better."

Back onboard, I was enjoying cake and hot tea when someone exclaimed, "Dolphins!" Through the wide windows, four dolphins were escorting us out of the bay. Beside me stood Carlos, the guide who'd presented a slide show on local birds. As a lifelong birder, I was curious about the seabirds crisscrossing ahead of the ship. "Black-browed albatross," he said, "and the black ones with white chests are imperial cormorants. They're migrating north now."

I added them to my list.

Our ship wove through the network of islands and fjords, rocking gently, and turned east into the Beagle Channel, bordering southern Tierra del Fuego, and another encounter with a history-making voyage. Naturalist Charles Darwin sailed these same waters on the research ship HMS *Beagle*, captained by Robert Fitzroy. Darwin's observations on this journey became the basis for his theory of evolution. On January 28, 1833, on night watch in the channel, Darwin wrote in his diary, "[T]here is something very solemn in such scenes; the consciousness rushes on the mind in how remote a corner of the globe you are in. . . ." I wanted to tell him, *I'm there with you.*

On our left rose the Darwin Cordillera, source of the looming glaciers along Glacier Alley. I fear that the glaciers face the fate of the Yaghan tribes, who once navigated their bark canoes in these waters bordering the island of Tierra del Fuego, but most of whom succumbed to European-introduced diseases.

That night I peered out the cabin window into the blackness and imagined seeing their distant fires, for which the island was named. There were no fires now.

"Much rocking in the night," I wrote. Yet we were up early the next day, for the Patagonian winds had calmed, and the captain gave the go-ahead for that day's excursion. The zodiacs carried us to a rocky shore, where we disembarked and climbed 160 steps to a level plain. With a life jacket strapped around my layers of fleece and waterproof parka, I waddled penguin-like along the damp boardwalk. Orange life jackets contrasted sharply with the terrain: pewter sea, gray sky, and ochre, green, and beige low vegetation. Euphoria washed over me. I was standing on the island of Cape Horn.

As I gazed south across the vast Drake Sea, the desolate grayness reminded me of Robert Scott's tragic Antarctic expedition. In spite of the severe hardships Scott and his party faced, he kept a meticulous journal until the day he died: of logistics, routes, his men's conditions, blizzards, ice packs, penguins, and whales. A search party eight months later found Scott and two companions in their frozen tent. Beneath Scott's body lay his notebooks. Such determination even in the face of death is the stuff of heroes. They were willing to sacrifice everything in pursuit of a dream. To do so demanded conviction, though never total certainty. Certainty is a rare visitor to our days. Our lives consist of multiple decisions lacking sureness, small daily acts of courage. Heroes' stories like these can inspire us to remain open to the unknown.

Our ship's contingent wended its way along the boardwalk to the albatross monument, honoring the sailors who lost their lives navigating these turbulent waters. Translated from Spanish, the inscription read:

I, the albatross that awaits at the end of the world
I am the forgotten soul of the sailors lost,
Rounding Cape Horn from all the seas of the world,
But die they did not in the fierce waves,
For today towards eternity, in my wings they soar,
In the last crevice of the Antarctic winds.

We stood there, buffeted by the wind, pondering those solemn words reminding us of the ultimate sacrifice given by those who came before to this desolate, wondrous landscape. Not words of consolation for the dead so much as a call to us to know that nature can offer solace even in the wildest places.

As we headed toward the lighthouse, Antaris, a large, wet German shepherd, ran to greet us. He lived in the home adjacent to the lighthouse with a Chilean naval officer, his wife, and their son. The officer welcomed our group of visitors in muddy boots. For a year, he would tend the lighthouse and keep a record of ship traffic. We bade them farewell, I, for one, impressed by the family's willingness to face the isolation and loneliness.

The following afternoon, we disembarked on Navarino Island at tranquil Wulaia Bay, where the Yaghan people once had everything they needed: forests, game, streams, and a protected bay for moving about in their canoes and diving for shellfish. Here, Captain Fitzroy returned Jemmy Button—one of the three natives the captain had taken to England on his previous voyage—to his people.

We hiked to a hilltop lookout through a forest red, orange, and yellow, glowing in the late-afternoon sunlight. I imagined that I saw diaphanous figures, the spirits of those people, moving silently among the trees, keening for their lost lands. Their self-identity was tightly bound with this, the only place they'd ever known as home. We can never mend the wrongdoing that led to their extermination, but we can respect this site in honor of those lost tribes.

Although I have had the option to put down my roots in many places, only one natural habitat, the place where I grew up, *feels* like home to me and tugs at me wherever I happen to be. I wonder about the more than half of the world's population who dwell in cities. Amid the distractions of city life, how difficult to maintain their inner attachment and respect for the natural landscape, once home to all of us. Even beyond city limits, television, computers, and cell phones can blind us to nature's wonders.

Dark clouds frowned overhead as our ship turned into Fiordo Chico, dotted with floating miniature ice sculptures. Two small birds perched on a gelid chunk, pecking at the ice. I hunched in the zodiac, rain and sleet stinging my face. My "water repellent" pants clung to my thermal underwear, which in turn cleaved to my legs like giant black leeches. *This is nothing,* I thought, *compared with the hardships of Magellan's malnourished crew.* No one offered them hot chocolate laced with whiskey on their return from a shore expedition.

Dusk. Our last day. From the upper deck, under a sky with clouds streaked coral and rose, I bade farewell to this wild scene and to Magellan, certain that he and his frightened sailors found hope in a flaming sunset and respite in the sheltering inlets of the straits. We must remember them and feel gratitude for those men with the foresight and inspiration to chronicle their journeys, and for that determined captain who opened the way for future travelers through this convoluted passage to the Pacific. There, Pigafetta reported that the captain, upon realizing their feat, "wept for joy." I understood. Five hundred years later, the wonder of this place could trigger the same emotions.

Patagonia: By Land and by Sea

Rain, thunder, and lightning visited us some days ago. A welcome rain, but short-lived. In Chile's dry, Atacama Desert region in the north, the driest in the world, entire small-town neighborhoods were wiped out by sudden, torrential rainfall and immense mudslides, while in the southern, water-deprived rain forests a massive fire rages, requiring importation of firefighters from neighboring countries. Earlier in the month, the Villarrica volcano flared up into a fiery eruption. All this in the month of March. It's beginning to look like Ursula Le Guin's science-fiction world. I feel the future rushing toward us like a fast-moving train. World events reinforce that sensation.

In the present of her novel *The Lathe of Heaven*, all the world's mountains have lost their eternal snows, even Mount Erebus, an active volcano in Antarctica. In *our* present, Santiago and I are cruising once again the gelid fjords of southern Patagonia, flanked by receding glaciers, amid ice floes and marine wildlife. I hope Ursula Le Guin was mistaken in her vision of a future with bare, glacier-less mountain ranges. Maybe, if I pay close attention, I'll hear the glaciers' whisperings and advice on their preservation.

Our zodiac speeds past ice sculptures floating on the steely surface of a bay, taking us to the base of the Brookes Glacier. It creaks and growls as it shifts on its granite perch. Turquoise columns break off the glacier and thunder into the bay. Again and again. I watch in absolute wonder. And I listen. Yes, I hear you, mountains. Your message is clear: *We are impenetrable. Immovable. You are just passing through.*

The ship turns back to the main channel of the Strait of Magellan, where young, sleek seals frolic in successive arched leaps, as if imitating dolphins. Is there anything as white as a seagull's breast? Yes. The absolute whiteness of the Darwin Cordillera in the Beagle Channel, home to more than six hundred glaciers, some still unnamed. I watch with alarm the torrents of melted ice rushing from the edges of the glaciers into the channel, reminding me that these masses are not eternal. A full, yellowy moon glimmers in our wake as we navigate through the last of Glacier Alley. The snowy Cordillera fades into the distance, and I try to imprint the memories of this scene in my mind so that I can revisit them as often as I wish.

From the green rising and falling swells of the fjords we return to terra firma to visit once more Torres Del Paine National Park. Two green and red *charanga* parrots peek at us out of their tree house home-in-a-hole.

The beauty of glacier-carved peaks towering over teal Lake Nordenskjöld heightens the tragedy of the bleached bones of skeleton forests we pass through. All around us looms the stark landscape recently devoured by a man-made forest fire. But, through my despair, I notice the green shoots of recuperating shrubs and grasses. Last night it rained, and today I breathe in the grateful fragrances of wet vegetation.

I have long wanted to visit a working Patagonian sheep ranch, so we've arranged to stay at the Estancia Tercera Barranca ranch. East of the park, we joggle and bounce along the dirt road winding through the wide expanses of pampa, populated by tufts of beige grass and prickly, tough black shrubs. Sheep graze behind fences that pose no obstacle to the long-legged guanacos. Rocky bluffs rise in the distance.

Dusk is approaching, and we welcome the sight of the

glittering lights of the estancia in the distance. A sense of adventure washes through me as we drive toward the only lights in these vast grasslands.

Nancy shows us our room, puts more logs on the fire in the living room, and explains that the generator is turned off at 11:00 p.m. After that, no lights and no heat. It is a chilly night.

A stone path leads to the separate kitchen–dining area, warm and fragrant, where Carmen, in a white chef's hat, serves us a savory salmon dinner with homegrown vegetables. Nancy and Carmen pamper us, the only two guests, and tell us their stories.

I've come to see the sheep and the gauchos, I tell them.

Oh, the sheep have been taken to another estancia to be "bathed," they explain, to be disinfected for ticks. We've come all this way and no sheep? Seeing my disappointment, they assure me the sheep will come back the day we leave.

The next day, we pick our way through the prickly shrubbery to climb a rocky bluff, from which the pampa stretches endlessly in all directions. The vastness of these plains strikes me as a mirror image of the southern seas that wash the shores of this continent.

Ready to leave the following day, I hear the shouts of the gauchos in the distance and run outside. Here comes what I've been waiting for—a moving, woolly mass flows wavelike over a low rise, heading for its home pasture. I'm disappointed that this is all I'll be able to see.

A wide, benevolent sky spreads out over the open pampa of grazing sheep and guanacos. We feel fortunate on this visit, as the weather in these southern climes can be harsh and unpredictable. We bid farewell to this landscape under a smiling sky.

After our return to the city, newscasts report dark, turbulent skies unleashing a two-day torrential deluge in the area we just left; it isolated ranchers, engorged rivers, and washed away hundreds of sheep.

Though I know that this is a land of extremes, it continues to shock and surprise. Last month, the news carried scenes of massive mudslides in Chile's northern desert region and raging fires in southern forests. This week, without any warning, the Calbuco volcano, inactive for forty-five years, spews skyward columns of red-hot lava and gigantic, lightning-pierced clouds of ash and stone. Ash and gravel settle in thick layers on nearby villages, farms, roads, and fields. Locals are evacuated until it's deemed safe for them to return to their homes. Television transmits scenes of horses searching in vain for food under the rubble and people shoveling gravel off their roofs to prevent their collapse before the announced rains. Beehives are being trucked to uncontaminated countryside.

Weathermen check the direction of the winds, which carry ash again into Argentina. Plane flights are canceled. All this just a few weeks after the Villarrica volcano erupted. These days, news anchors interview volcanologists and geologists to cultivate public understanding and dispel incorrect theories: volcanoes are all connected underground; unusual weather signals the advent of an earthquake. All old wives' tales, but it's easy to understand their origins: wherever you go in this long, thin country, the land trembles.

This meteorological, tectonic turbulence strikes me as Earth's reminder that we inhabit a living planet. We must never forget how vulnerable we are. Life here is never dull. I love the rough edges of this land, which allow me to feel like an adventurer. Beyond the city lies nature at its rawest. It beckons to me.

Island Footprints

The purring launch carries us across the teal waters of Puyehue Lake, in Chile's Patagonia. We are returning to the island of Fresia, after a lapse of many years. There will be changes, but I hope the essence of the place remains as I remember. . . .

Earth

We follow the steep path leading to the peak, a traditional island hike. In places overgrown with grass and wild bamboo, we lose our way, making our own trail, bending the tall stalks with our feet. Thick forests of laurel, arrayán, and wild fuchsia alternate with open meadows, alive with small orange butterflies. The loud cry of a flicker stops us in our tracks. Binoculars lifted, we spot his speckled shape on an overhead branch. Rivulets of spring water trickle into shady depressions on the trail. Behind us, we leave footprints, that marking of our passing in the soil that is denied to city dwellers. I think of Wallace Stegner's affirmation: "Wearing any such path in the earth's rind is an intimate act, an act like love . . . an opportunity that few any longer can have. . . ."

We stop to take in the vast panorama of the lake, set against the backdrop of craggy Andean peaks, a landscape molded and carved by restless tectonic plates, glaciers, and rumbling volcanoes. In the distance rises the cinder cone of the Caulle volcano, which has wreaked havoc all summer. Fine white ash covers every surface inside and outside the island house, while a massive patch of floating pumice spreads over the lake's surface. We venture out in the old launch, swerving to avoid floating logs, opening a path through the thick pumice carpet that tap-taps the sides of our vessel. The small beach used for swimming and sunbathing wears a mantle of the featherweight stones, deposited by the lake waters.

Water

Returning to the unpainted clapboard house, I feel as if I could drink a barrelful of the island water. Surging from the ground, it tastes of spring breath, crystalline, silken as it slides down my throat. I can't get enough.

Alone on the porch, rimmed by bright blue hydrangeas, I become aware of an unrelenting sound, the lapping of tongues of water at the shore below. I try to imagine the monolithic glacier that sculpted this vessel, this valley, causing the cerulean waters to pause in their flow from mountain to sea.

Rain is always lurking beyond the horizon here. The abundant precipitation is the greening force of this landscape, nourishing the lush vegetation, ferns, and mosses, feeding hillside springs and puddles where birds can quench their thirst. It flows in the veins of the island, lending freshness to all, bluing the skies and cleansing the air.

Air

Here, I drink from a well of silence. Yet the air is never completely still. Leaves murmur. A hummingbird's wings whir nearby. I miss the goose-like honk of the native ibis, no longer an island inhabitant, thanks to the introduction of minks, with their predilection for birds' eggs. Nor do we hear the teasing cry of the *chucao*, the emblematic bird of Chile's southern rain forests.

From the kitchen window drifts the aroma of freshly baked brown bread, irresistible, the perfect morning companion to homemade raspberry jam and a mug of coffee. I remember I have a similar bread recipe at home and vow to make it in the upcoming cooler days of fall. It's worth the effort just to fill my house with that scent.

Billowing, flat-bottomed clouds sail across the sky, but the day is warm and we take the path to the horseshoe-shaped beach, with a swim on our minds. Yesterday at the beach alone, I spotted a perky kingfisher flitting from rock to branch, eyes intent on the calm waters. Here he is again, and I call to the others. Posing on a bare branch, he seems to enjoy the attention, his feathers ruffling in the wind. We talk of the utter peace of this place and watch the changing water and sky. The wind is gaining force now, piling up blackening clouds, turning the lake waters into a palette of grays. Draped in our towels, we scurry back to the house, anxious for a warming fire.

Fire

In the living room, we kneel before the tall woodburning stove. My friend and I poke at the branches and logs, feeding them with shreds of paper. "We need more tinder wood," I say. I am not about to concede that I've lost my Girl Scout fire-starting skills. Soon the logs ignite, and we watch with pleasure the flicker of the flames through the glass window.

The woodburning stoves in these damp southern climes can be friend or foe. Earlier this morning, I walked through the overgrown remains of the house where we stayed on our first visit. Several years ago, it burned to the ground when someone failed to close the stove door tightly. I remember how the house's owner, Señora Liese, showed us to our room, which held two beds covered with white, hand-sewn goose-down quilts. Wood was the protagonist throughout: floors, walls, beds, chairs, tables, bookshelves, even the shower stalls—all hand-crafted. On a windowsill stood a small vase of wildflowers. I felt transported back to the pioneer days of the 1930s, when European immigrants, like Liese, settled in southern Chile. Now I lamented the loss—the craftsmanship, the history the house held—as I tried to determine where that bedroom once stood.

In the evening, we warm up slices of bread on racks in an upper oven, enclosed by two iron doors. Gathered around the table, we create our own sandwiches with cheese, cold cuts, avocado, and tomatoes. Except for the bread and a lemon pie, all this food was ferried from the local market, unlike our previous visit, when the island families were largely self-sufficient.

Solar panels now provide electricity during the day, but at dusk we light candles while waiting for the generator to be turned on. Outside, all is not darkness. From a break in the sweeping clouds, a brilliant full moon spills a silvery path across the water.

Midnight. I crawl under the eiderdown and reach for my book, Stegner's *Wolf Willow*, about his homesteader boyhood on the plains of Saskatchewan, an environment starkly opposed to my present, verdant surroundings. Yet this pioneer-built home on Fresia most likely began as a shack like Stegner's, constructed by men's hard labor in an inclement climate.

The lights flicker and die. They've turned off the generator. The wood floors creak as others ready for bed. I switch on my headlamp and read until my eyelids grow heavy.

Now, on this early, crisp morning already hinting at fall, I step out into my city garden and breathe in deeply. Closing my eyes, I recall the translucent island air, and, for a few moments, I am there.

V. A WORLD OF WORDS

My Roget's Thesaurus *and I are inseparable. It informs me that I am a logophile—a lover of words. I embrace their multiple meanings and uses and sounds. Gleeful gladiolas, riotous revelry. Magnificent metaphors and sly similes, allusions and delusions, hysterical hyperbole and holy hosannas. A scene of beauty, a moment of ecstasy, a spark of understanding—on the wings of words, all can be revealed: the incredible silkiness of an owl feather, the trill of a canary, the tingle of a hot pepper, a watermelon sunset, the heady scent of spring's first acacia blooms.*

Current

Current affairs occupied a slot in our curriculum at St. Anselm's Grammar School in the 1950s. The class subscribed to a newsletter, *My Weekly Reader*. We looked forward to its arrival every Friday. The nuns also encouraged us to cut out newspaper articles that piqued our interest at home and report on them to the class. Those memories stuck with me.

Only in the past two decades have Internet and cable channels given me a direct line to instantaneous news here in Chile. For many years, my only source of US and world news was the local newspaper, which was subject to censorship under the military dictatorship. Now I'm a current-events junkie, reading the news online and the local newspaper front to back and checking the CNN international news cable channel at least twice a day. The result has been a sharp rise in my worry-level indicator. First, it was the global economy. Then the 2008 and 2016 US presidential elections had me on the edge of my seat. And the tension never lets up: terrorism, wars, refugees, famine. I mustn't forget climate change and natural disasters: hurricanes, tsunamis, earthquakes, forest fires, floods. And now, here in Chile, volcanic eruptions bury farms and roads under tons of ash and gravel.

Why do I want to know all this? Why *watch* the suffering?

Because I am a part of this global community we call humanity. I consider myself a public citizen, which I believe carries the responsibility of keeping informed and participating. Locally, I am involved with our neighborhood association, which was key in blocking the construction of a mall nearby, a powerful example of grassroots democracy.

But on the international level, it's easy to feel powerless. What happens worldwide sends off ripples that reach the most distant shores. I feel like a fish carried along by strong ocean currents, or like a butterfly buffeted by the wind. World events, like the wind, continuously change direction and force, soon becoming history to make space for more recent news demanding my attention. It is easy to feel hopeless.

But the news also tells me we are *not* helpless. We have used our intelligence to develop mind-boggling technological and scientific advances. We now can harness the forces of the ocean, the sun, and the wind in a move toward living in greater harmony with nature. Yet the solutions allowing *cultures* to live in harmony remain elusive and complex.

Seldom is one person alone capable of changing the course of events, but it is possible. Peace, respect, and compassion have faces: Gandhi, Nelson Mandela, Martin Luther King, Mother Teresa. But we can't all be public heroes. My circumstances limit me to sending off prayers, signing endless online petitions, donating a bit here and there, and posting campaigns on Facebook. I strive to cultivate those values within my individual spheres and join with others to form a massive positive force.

The written word possesses sublime power and can remove us from the continuous Internet-and-television barrage of information and advertising. Opening a book, we enter a realm of quiet and thoughtfulness. As an elementary school teacher, I have read many awe-inspiring children's books, whose authors have given us some magnificent, lasting lessons in generous, respectful living: Barbara Cooney's *Miss Rumphius*, about a planter of lupine seeds in the wild who creates a wondrous lavender world; Shel Silverstein's *The Giving Tree*, about an oak tree capable of selfless giving; Leo Lionni's *Swimmy*, about a little red fish who teaches other small fish that a community is stronger if it sticks together. If those books were required reading for every child and adult, to be read not once, but again and again, this earth would be a more harmonious place.

And now I will toss these lupine-seed words to the wind. May they take root and bloom far and wide.

A Bookworm's Dilemma

I never thought I'd be saying this, but I have to admit it now: Kindle is a great invention. A plethora of books in English are accessible with the tap of a finger to this eager reader living in a non-English-speaking country. Thanks to this device, I'm reading more than ever: fiction and nonfiction, exploring authors previously unknown to me, recommended books, Pulitzer Prize winners. I read not only for pleasure but also to learn more of the writing craft. I read more critically. Some authors disappoint me, but if they enjoy wide acclaim, I don't give up on them. I may encounter within the pages a bit of illumination that renders the effort worthwhile.

When I discover an author whose writing I love, I want to read more. This happened after I read Geraldine Brooks's book *March*, a novel about Mr. March, the father of the girls in *Little Women*. What a clever idea to imagine the life of a secondary character in a famous novel. I then realized that I remembered scarcely any of *Little Women* and would like to read it again. I wonder what happened to the faded blue hardcover copy that belonged to my mother.

This started me thinking of other books I'd like to reread: L. M. Montgomery's *Anne of Green Gables*, John Steinbeck's *Travels with Charley*, Marilynne Robinson's *Gilead*. Then a doubt haunts me: Should I spend time rereading when there is so much out there that I have never read?

It was well worth rereading *One Hundred Years of Solitude*, *Ishi in Two Worlds*, and *Blue Highways*, but, more than all others, I return again and again to Amy Leach's *Things That Are*. I make lists of her goofy, wonderful word combinations, as well as invented terms, like "jewel-babblers" and "botherations," reading them over in the hope that some of her magic will rub off on me. I'd be desolate without my hard copy.

Yes, I still prefer the *real* thing—the book in my hands, my fingers turning the pages, underlining brilliant thoughts or beautifully expressed ideas. In the twentieth century, a rich culture grew up around books. I still have books that belonged to my mother, who proclaimed her ownership with a black-and-white bookplate that read, "Ex Libris," followed by her name. Inside the front page, she wrote, "If this book should chance to roam, box its ears and send it home," below which she wrote her address.

I still have bookplates I bought in high school that bear the image *The Great Wave off Kanagawa*, by Japanese artist Hokusai. "From the Library of . . ." is followed by a space for my name. I'd forgotten I had these bookplates. Does anyone use bookplates anymore? Is it that readers seldom buy hard copies and keep them now, but pass them on to others? When I finish a book, if I decide it's a keeper, I'll squeeze it onto a bulging bookshelf. I like the thought of gluing a bookplate into my favorite books and imagining that someone years from now will know that I cherished that volume.

I particularly love books with a strong sense of place—like Ivan Doig's and William Stegner's books. If the place is one I have visited or plan to visit, my journey is all the richer. Soon, I'll be visiting St. Petersburg. Having just read Rosemary Sullivan's *Stalin's Daughter*, I'm already in a Russian state of mind. Years ago, I found Edward Rutherfurd's *Russka* fascinating. Perhaps a reread to brush up on my history? Or a Tolstoy or Dostoyevsky that I haven't read? My options are endless.

Nicanor Parra Turns One Hundred

This is a country that venerates its poets, and this month celebrations are in order. Nicanor Parra, Chile's *anti-poeta*, is turning one hundred years old. I visit a photographic exhibit in his honor and am surprised to notice a photo of him visiting the University of California, Berkeley. He was invited by Chilean professor Fernando Alegría, with whom I studied Latin American literature there. Just two degrees of separation!

At the exhibit, I learn that Nicanor, from a talented, humble family, was a mathematician and physicist until he studied in England. There, he read Shakespeare and classic English poetry, whereupon he did a complete turnabout and published his first book, *Poems and Anti-poems*. He became an inspiration for Beat poet Allen Ginsberg. After his recitations, he would say, "I take back everything I said."

A second exhibition seems an authentic reflection of Parra's playful, astute personality, featuring a diverse sampling of his newspaper headline collages and illustrated quotes. "Thought dies in the mouth" is my favorite. I laugh at the humor, irony, and irreverence in his display of artifacts, common items with quirky labels: a roll of soft toilet paper labeled "bourgeoisie," alongside newspaper squares for the "proletariat," a Coke bottle labeled "message in a bottle," a bunch of unmatched socks. His talent for playing with words is evident in one of my favorite quotes (translated): "Read from back to front, to the contrary, nothing happens." Can he mean that, approaching the written word from different directions or angles or mindsets, you can be in for a surprise? I leave the exhibit stimulated but questioning my ability to write with irreverence or irony.

Writers must be patient. Inspiration and ideas aren't instantly on call. I must *wait.* My mind is like alphabet soup, letters and nascent words floating about, seeking coherence and something worthwhile. I stir the chaotic brew and let random ideas mull. Often when I'm out for a walk, the kernel of an idea surfaces, or, like today, while I watered my houseplants, I knew I wanted to write something inspired by my visit with Parra and read more of his anti-poems.

As much as I love to read his anti-poems, I must acknowledge that I doubt I can write in Nicanor's ironic style, so different from my writer's voice. Would I want to? It would definitely be out of character, but I might discover untried creative juices. His poems feel like a dare. Dare to be different.

Nicanor Parra passed away on January 24, 2018, the same day as Ursula Le Guin.

Los Parronales Writing Retreat

A "country mouse, city mouse" syndrome is my unshakeable phantom. I long for the countryside but am destined to big-city living. But now I have a precious break: our annual writers' retreat-workshop at Los Parronales farm. I settle into my room and walk to the window, which frames a wide field edged by trees.

Paying Attention

I open myself to sounds: twittering quail, blackbirds chattering, airplanes passing, a tractor tilling the field across the road, the wind swooshing through the eucalyptus trees like ocean waves—roaring, then hushing.

Outside, lying on my back, I see: a true-blue sky, a seed fairy, a small yellow butterfly buffeted by the wind and struggling to stay on course, soaring hawks. At eye level, bees and butterflies sample pollen.

In the fading light of dusk, I notice: a horned-owl family perched in the eucalyptus tree where I've spotted them in previous years. The gaggle of writers comes out for a look.

In bed I hear: crickets, distant barking dogs, rowdy lapwings sounding the alarm.

Owls

Four solemn *tucuqueres*, or lesser horned owls, perched in the eucalyptus tree, have we writers entranced. I now have a feather memento. Silky soft. I attempt a photo of the owls with my cell phone, but the light is wrong. I'll try again in the morning. The owls seem totally unperturbed by gawking writers and this bumbling photographer crashing in the underbrush.

Canadian writer-editor-publisher Beth Follett entitles her morning workshop session "Relinquishing Fear." She is referring to our personal writing practices and the inner fears that get in the way. She reads to us from Alice Munro and poets Dionne Brand and Don McKay. We explore the many meanings of "wilderness."

Lunch on the terrace with the brown Central Valley hills behind us, followed by a lovely, complete switch. Beth's husband, poet Stan Dragland, plays his Washburn Rover guitar, and he and Beth sing Dolly Parton's "Wildflowers." Love it. This rich environment of words, lyrics, poetry, stories, and song fills me. What will I do with it?

I've been out to view the owls several times today (as have the others) and have returned to sit in my quiet (except for the country birdsong) bedroom—my writer's cell. For now, I will read and think and see where all this takes me.

Manure

Through my window drifts the soughing of the wind and the lowing of cows. Cows bring to mind cow plops and *manure*. I write the word in italics as a sign of reverence. Yes, reverence.

Earlier, out walking along the dirt road bordering the fields, I smelled that sweet scent. It's a pleasant fragrance to me, evoking other rural places I've known. I particularly recall the two interludes I spent as an adolescent at a Girl Scout camp referred to as "primitive." Situated near the town of Sierraville in a high cattle-raising valley of California, it was a place devoid of any constructions, except a storage hut. We slept on the open ground, dug our own latrines, and cooked our food over campfires. I remember walking with caution to the creek so we didn't step in any cow patties.

Manure . . . reverence. One of the books I brought along is Wendell Berry's *Imagination in Place.* I wanted to read Berry after learning he is a poet, writer, grower, and environmentalist. In an essay dedicated to his poet friend Hayden Carruth, he refers to the poem "Marshall Washer," about a dairy farmer in Vermont. Apparently, New England farmers sometimes refer to themselves as "cowshit farmers."

Carruth wrote:

*Notice how many times
I have said "manure"? It is serious business.
It breaks the farmers' backs. It makes their land.
It is the link eternal, binding man and beast and earth.*

Carruth wants us to know that it is by returning the manure to the fields that these farmers are involved in the fertility cycle, allowing the fields to be cultivated so that the living world can eat. "Cowshit," then, says Berry, is "the link eternal."

This is a big, awesome thought—one to carry with me as I walk the aisles of the supermarket, far from fields and the scent of *manure.*

On Being Alone

Still at Los Parronales, working at learning the craft of writing. Our poet-writer mentors are fine-tuning our listening, observation, and thinking skills, pushing us to go deeper, make connections and discoveries, shine our light on new truths. Poets' lines shimmer, suspended in the air, waiting for us to absorb their brilliance and simplicity.

Reading material is scattered about our large worktable. The title of an article attracts my attention: "Why Do We Have

Such a Problem with Being Alone?" A photograph shows the author, Sara Maitland, standing alone on a high Scottish moor, gazing into the distance. For the past twenty years, she has lived alone in an isolated place. She examines what she calls a "serious cultural problem"—society's attitude toward solitude and common assumptions that it is self-indulgent, escapist, antisocial, and an evasion of social responsibility.

I am relieved to discover someone who questions society's judgments on being alone, particularly that it is antisocial. When I lean back in my chair and tune out at an especially noisy event, I worry I'm being a lone wolf. That's what a teacher colleague called me once years ago. It felt like a black mark on my forehead, a label I believed I didn't deserve. Growing up an only child, I was used to solitude and silences. Sometimes that also meant loneliness, but "alone" isn't necessarily equivalent to "lonely." I prefer going to a movie or concert accompanied, but I'm not reluctant to go by myself.

Here at the workshop, I have a room of my own. Sitting at my desk, I hear the footsteps of others and the wind in the eucalyptus and cottonwood trees—delicious solitude, but I am not alone.

Farewell

Following the farewell barbecue, Ian and Solange, two local teenagers dressed in traditional dress, perform the cueca folk dance for us. My throat tightens, and tears well. Am I becoming sentimental about Chile? I think it is a sense of impending loss—a tragic loss for Chilean culture, as well as for us, who may never be treated to this joyful tradition again. Such pride in their young faces, the boy stomping his black boots, spurs jangling, the girl twirling coquettishly around him, swirling a white kerchief in the air. In this small farming community, few remain to carry on the country traditions: the horsemanship, the music, the dancing. Spreading urbanization—industries and massive storage lots for new imported cars—is devouring the fields that produce grapes, tomatoes, alfalfa, and prickly pear fruit. Cars outnumber horses and cattle. Alfalfa, furrowed soil, and weeping willows are retreating before the march of metal, glass, and plastic. Where will the owl family find refuge?

VI. ASKING THE QUESTIONS

As we mature, we slowly develop our own particular philosophy of life. At thirty or forty or fifty, we may ask, What kind of person do I want to be? *Around about sixty, we might find that the question shifts:* What kind of person am I becoming? *We reach an awareness that the "becoming" part is lifelong.*

To find answers, we must first decide the questions we want to ask: What is important to me? How can I help make this world a better place? What must I do to become the person I want to be?

Small, everyday moments often reveal answers to our existential questions.

Leaf

Every particular in nature, a leaf, a drop, a crystal, a moment of time is related to the whole, and partakes of the perfection of the whole. —Ralph Waldo Emerson

The autumnal equinox occurred last week, but I hardly took notice. Our days have been exceptionally warm for mid-March. Yet small signs are here: the return of the hummingbirds; fresh, brisk mornings; shorter days; and, of course, the leaves. Below one tree lies a scattering of round, lemony leaves, just the start of the tree's shedding. The higher leaves of the liquidambar next door are blushing scarlet. Earlier today, a gaggle of brown, papery leaves scurried noisily down the street on a gust of wind. Where were they off to?

We will not sweep up the garden leaves. Not yet. I enjoy looking at them—their colors and their disarray.

I can think of definite advantages of the ability to shed—to discard, like a snake, the old skin for a new one—but I must reconcile myself to an inner shedding, a letting-go. It's scary and uncomfortable to look within for what I need to wrench out—those tough, persistent weeds: shreds of old angers and resentments, lingering guilt, useless regrets, life's detritus and vanities.

But how? I look to the leaves. No holding back there. They freely abandon their perches on branch and twig to mix with the soil below. It's hibernation time for trees, a turning inward to store energy for a season of new growth. No leaf or tree focuses on itself; it simply follows Mother Nature's plan. If I turn my attention away from self, toward the great oneness of which I am a part, then perhaps I, too, can feel an unburdening.

Leaf by leaf.

Lost: One Green Thumb

Tiny, green, munching worms. Disfiguring tumors on my fuchsias. Browning rose leaves. Weed invasion on my lawn. Am I losing my touch? Or can I blame these garden afflictions on El Niño? He takes the blame for anything out of the ordinary, including welcome events like an abundance of butterflies this spring. Our ever-present air pollution is another convenient scapegoat. I must share some of the blame for garden failures and go through the checklist. Overwatering? Over- or under-fertilizing? Too much sunlight? Too much shade? The plant doesn't like its pot? I resort to garden books and the Internet for answers and nontoxic pesticides.

Today I discovered that gall mites are the culprits of my fuchsia woes. There it was. A photo online. "That's it!" I cried. Two plant experts had been unable to diagnose the problem. Now I must persevere and accept the challenge—cutting off the ugly, tumorlike protrusions and mixing a spray solution to be used weekly. The Internet expert warns that I may never totally eliminate the mites, as hummingbirds and bees spread them. Imagine a garden without those visitors.

My persevering care last year paid off with Speedy Gonzalez, our sick tortoise. Syringe feeding for months, blood tests, and X-rays were onerous and time-consuming, and offered no guarantee of success. I'm pleased to report that he's back to his old tortoise self this season, pacing the backyard, munching grass greedily, and gorging on fallen apricots, occasionally sneaking into the house.

Our hopes and endeavors may or may not bear fruit. That's the challenge that enriches us—not knowing the outcome.

Persistence in the face of uncertainty. Russian writer Anna Akhmatova regarded living as a "habit." This idea had me thinking—for about sixty seconds. Yes, habit does occupy a certain part of my days. But what about the conscious decisions I make throughout the day, decisions that require effort, like treating an ailing tortoise or planning a birthday getaway for my husband? If life consisted only of habit, how boring our days would be. What of our efforts? Achievements? Failures? Why get up in the morning if no elements of serendipity or surprise are possible or even probable?

A brief event today reminded me always to expect the unexpected, for a state of constant expectation is the antithesis of habit. I went to my Pilates class, my usual morning routine three days a week, where we often discuss our aches and ailments and recommend treatments. Afterward, the supermarket was on my schedule. But Yolanda, a Pilates colleague and neighbor, invited me to her house, where she massaged my arthritic wrists and thumbs with her miraculous oils. Bliss! She covered my wrists with her hands, transmitting her warmth, and then followed up with a soothing massage. I told her how wonderful it was to feel her caring touch. She sent me home with a bottle of cannabis oil—on loan. Maybe I'll recover my lost green thumb.

Check

Life consists of what man is thinking all day.
—Ralph Waldo Emerson

Opening my eyes to the first morning light: What day is it? Yesterday was Tuesday, so this must be Wednesday. What does the day have in store? Pilates class and then the grocery store. Better get a move on.

Before I go: take my pills; brush my teeth; apply deodorant, moisturizer, and sunblock. Earrings? Got them. Don't forget to feed the tortoise. Put cell phone in purse. Water the rosebush. On my way to the supermarket, I worry: Did I lock the house? Bring my shopping list and my bags? Check.

At the supermarket: lock the car, tip the bag girl, remember the receipt for the plastic Coke bottle. Make a mental meal plan. Tonight and tomorrow: Swiss chard pancakes. Friday: fish (check if they have sea bass). Weekend: corn pie. Monday and Tuesday: stuffed zucchini. Plums for the tortoise. Check.

Back home: Daniel, our current gardener, comes this afternoon. Ask him to pull weeds, trim the ivy, fertilize the sequoia and the fuchsias, cut dead flowers from the buddleia. Check. Check. Check.

At my desk: piles of paper clamor for attention. Unrelenting reminders. File those, shelve this, scan and email that. Tomorrow, the writing group meets. I need to whip out something for the Tuesday prompt; the word is "check."

Once dinner is ready and the day is cooling, the mental lists agitate less, brain activity slows. I watch the news but wake with a jolt of my drooping head. Suddenly I remember—still must print the Tuesday prompt for tomorrow. Check.

In bed: Did I take all my pills? Lock the back door? Turn off the computer? Check. Check. Check.

No wonder I drop off to sleep in front of the television at night. Not only is my body tired, but my brain is as well. That miraculous organ pulsating behind my eyes and protected by my skull *never* stops. If I pause to examine its inner workings, what do I discover? Checklists! Multiple reminders for everyday living.

Sigh. Tomorrow, I'll leave space for some creative moments. The day may have twenty-four hours, but my mind has no such limitations. I can handle more than checklists. Now that I'm retired from teaching, my inner voice reminds me how precious time is, so I consider carefully how I want to spend it. My days might include Pilates classes, cooking, pruning a rosebush, or signing online political petitions. Today, I look forward to several pleasurable moments: reading my book club's assigned book, Maya Angelou's *I Know Why the Caged Bird Sings*; taking a walk while pondering an essay title and writing a blog piece. And then there's the contentment that will come when I slip between the sheets tonight, having accomplished all that, plus my checklists. I reward myself with more of Angelou.

Unloading

Today is International Recycling Day, according to our local newspaper, which included a special supplement on the subject. Also included were heavy, glossy magazines from department stores and a travel agency, one dedicated entirely to sweaters, and another to the latest in giant TVs, promising the same sensation as actually *being* at the upcoming World Cup in Brazil.

I took a big load today to our local recycling center, not because it's International Recycling Day. I'm just tying up loose ends before we travel to New York tomorrow. I expected a line at the recycling center, but I was the only one there.

Preparing for a trip does weird things to my head. I feel the need to put order in my life and our house, rather like emptying an inbox labeled "Life." I clean up a pile of papers in my study—drafts and rewrites and more rewrites—which gives me a light, uncluttered feeling. I tackle the pile of papers to be shred. The shredder hums and grinds as I insert a 1988 income tax declaration, ancient bank statements, an old power of attorney. Yes! Out you go! What relief to have those papers out of my sight. I check the garden for any urgent last-minute snipping or spraying, respond to all pending emails and delete all the spam (over one hundred!), and buy boxes of pills to cover my medical needs for two weeks. I'll sort them into bags marked "a.m.," "p.m.," and "other."

Next on my list is choosing a lightweight paperback to read on the plane. I've read only half of *Cien Años de Soledad,* but this deluxe edition is way too heavy for travel. I do worry that when I return, I will have totally forgotten who is who among all the Aurelios and the Arcadios.

I could spend hours at the Strand bookstore in New York. But there's never enough time to browse, and then there's the tough decision of narrowing down my choices to what will fit in my suitcase.

"Narrowing down" is a must when traveling. And in life. What do I need? What are the essentials? For this trip? For my life? I feel a certain anxiety about leaving home, because it involves some uprooting, if only temporary. To travel, I must *leave behind* the known and the comfortable while I *go forth* to the novel, the stimulating and eye-opening. I am ready. Long stretches of time in this same urban routine stultify me, deadening my senses, my perceptions, my capacity for wonder.

New York City, here I come.

Living Gifts

On our second date, Santiago took me to my first track meet, and he was competing. Today, forty-five years and countless track competitions later, I turn down his offer to join him at yet another one, preferring to sit in my garden, patterned with shafts of a buttery fall sun. I no longer know the competitors, unlike years ago, when, as South America's four-hundred-meter hurdles champion, he kept me up to date on their names and records. When my two sons began competing, I burst with pride each time they stepped up to the winners' podium. Later, I lived the excitement of watching my men run the New York Marathon.

Before my introduction to track, there was opera. I dated an opera buff who helped train my ear to recognize and appreciate the voices of Renata Tebaldi and Maria Callas. We were present at the San Francisco Opera House when James McCracken lost his voice singing *Othello* yet completed the opera singing falsetto. Later, my husband and I enjoyed years of Santiago opera performances together. Maybe that operatic seed just needed encouragement to germinate, for as a child I followed Rudolph Bing's presentation of the New York Met Saturday performances on my wood-veneered, push-button Westinghouse radio while my mother listened on her own radio in the kitchen.

Family camping vacations alongside Glen Alpine Creek in the Sierra Nevada, fishing with my father at Lily Lake, and identifying birds visiting our backyard feeder made deep, lasting impressions during my childhood. Now, while vacationing with friends, Santiago and I infect them with our enthusiasm for bird watching, friends who previously couldn't distinguish a pelican from a penguin.

The passions of many people in my life have spilled over into me. They were unaware that they were giving me something, for it was intangible, not an object. I did nothing to earn these gifts and never said thank you because I recognized these shared passions as gifts only later in life. Now, as with bird watching, I've joined this cycle of reciprocity.

Grandparents are in a position to transmit their special interests to grandchildren, though often as a conscious act of *giving*. I haven't yet shown our family's three generations of stamp collections to my grandchildren. I'm waiting for the right moment, when there are no smartphones or iPads nearby. I once sent each an Easter card (though we live in the same city) so that they'd have the experience of receiving mail through the postal service. When they come to visit, they take out my gardening tools, gloves, and watering can to "work" in the garden with me. Or I suggest that they help me gather lemons from our backyard tree. Searching for sow bugs under rocks to save them in jars is another favorite pastime. What will they take away from these experiences?

Is that why I write? To share my sensations of awe, my reflections, my existential questions? Although I hope the reader finds meaning in my words, I have no idea what she will take away, and I expect nothing in return, but I like to imagine that my musings may spark a nod, a smile, or a tear, or recognition of a thing of beauty, like a small, burnished acorn.

Close Encounters

I only went out for a walk, and finally concluded to stay out till sundown, for going out, I found, was really going in.

—John Muir

A small, speckled spider crouched on the shower floor this morning. I cut the water, gently picked up the drenched critter with a square of toilet paper, and placed it on the outside window ledge. Slowly, it began to move its legs, and after my shower, it was gone. Did my rescue make any difference in the grand scheme of things? Probably not, but I hope it was able to continue on performing its spidery activities.

Living in Santiago, Chile, as with all big-city dwellers, we are limited to nonhuman visitors in the petite category. Strays frequently wander into our house, things that prefer to be out, rather than in. I'm happy to pluck up disoriented sow bugs and return them to their squirming clan in our garden. Lost ladybugs are definitely on my rescue list. Sometimes a small sparrow will hop through our open kitchen door in summer. Sparrows are cleverer than spiders at finding their way out.

Speedy Gonzalez, our tortoise, recently emerged from hibernation. In spite of his lengthy seclusion, he often tiptoes his way into our bedroom, squeezing into a corner under the radiator. I don't mind him there, but if I were he, I'd want to be outside. As he's not the expressive type, I have no way of knowing his thoughts on the subject. Although I do know that, as a native of the dry scrublands of the Argentine Patagonia, he was not designed for living in a walled city garden or under a radiator.

While visiting my small hometown in Northern California, I'm reminded that uninvited mammals can be a challenge, and that luring them out requires some guile. Take goats—they're not picky; they're happy in or out. I forget to close a door while staying with friends, and it's an open invitation to the neighbor's two free-roaming goats. With so many tempting things to nibble inside, they are not eager to follow me out. A granola bar finally provides sufficient motivation.

A gallivanting squirrel dislodges acorns from the oak tree outside my guest room window. *Plunk* onto the porch. He poses on his back haunches on the railing, the acorn clenched between his paws. He has competition for the acorns: wily woodpeckers and boisterous blue jays. In the past, they had to compete with the native peoples, who ground the acorns into meal, and with we kids, who wore the acorn caps on the tips of our small fingers.

I delight in frog encounters, whether at the New York Museum of Natural History's live exhibit, where I marvel at their kaleidoscope of colors: cerulean, hyacinthine, sage, sapphire, vermilion, topaz, chartreuse; or in the tropics, where their nighttime chorus in the rainy season resonates like a full orchestra; or in Tuscany at nightfall, as dozens of the small fellows line up at the edge of our brightly lit hotel pool to sing and demonstrate their underwater prowess with the frog kick; or on the shore of the Puelo River in Patagonia, where I spot a fingernail-size gray frog and am unable to resist picking him up and cupping him briefly in my palm.

For most creatures, it's a fuzzy line between in and out, this trespassing into what we humans consider our territory. Rascally raccoons live up to their bandito looks, sniffing their way to food and garbage, thinking nothing of a nighttime tiptoe across a kitchen counter, leaving telltale paw prints. We don't think twice about entering *their* domain, but I can't resist. I'm curious and want to get a close-up look at that bushy-tailed coyote staring across the farm fence at me. We're both wary yet interested. As are the three deer holding their staring stance in the dusky meadow, still as statues, except for their flicking white tails.

That's as far as our encounters go, for they are wild, which is what draws me to them. And it is their wildness that draws the line in our shared territories. Yet . . . I sense something crossing that line. That coyote and I are aware of our living, breathing Oneness.

VII. GRACE

Now more than ever, women's stories are more accessible to us. Their stories can be enlightening and poignant, or tragic and heartrending. In these narratives, some spend their days in domestic occupations—feeding backyard birds, making a pot of tea; an immigrant struggles with a new language; an aging woman calls upon her Maker to grant her strength; expatriates consider the nature of friendship. Yet all wear a cloak of unique feminine grace that bestows upon them compassion, wisdom, and resilience to face the challenges and capture the joys of their days.

Three Thimbles

The three thimbles in the palm of my hand catch the light from the window. Three thimbles from three women. I was the only girl, so they were handed on to me. The truth is, I'm all thumbs with a thimble, but I value these because they belonged to strong females who influenced my growing years.

One silver thimble, dainty like its owner, bears a delicate flower design and the filigreed initials BC, for Belle Cross, my maternal grandfather's sister. Aunty Belle, less than five feet tall, was a modest homemaker and steadfast wife to Uncle Will. As they had no children, my mother, their niece, faithfully drove south over the mountains to Santa Cruz, where they lived in an antique-filled Victorian cottage. My mother expected me to accompany her on these weekend outings. I did not look forward to the hour-and-a-half drive and the fact that once we arrived, there would be no children to play with. But Aunty Belle and Uncle Will were kind and affectionate, pleased to have their only grand-niece for a visit. I loved exploring the rooms of their house: shelves filled with books with titles embossed in gold, the kitchen pantry, the piano, the upstairs bedroom with the sloped ceiling, the backyard birdbath, and Uncle Will's tool shed. All smelled musty, though not unpleasant. Uncle Will was a radio repairman, so they lived frugally. I can picture Aunty Belle darning Uncle Will's socks, her wee middle finger capped with the silver thimble.

After Uncle Will's death, Aunty Belle, unassuming and self-contained, followed her long-established routines: attending Sunday church services, listening to the radio, inviting a neighbor in for tea and Scottish shortbread, and going about her household chores at a snail's pace. Breakfast of porridge, tea, and toast at her kitchen table could not be rushed. Her unhurried ways flow in my blood. As a child, I was a dreamer and a dawdler, consistently late for everything. Life's obligations forced me to quicken my pace, but in recent years I've reverted to my old ways, the memory of Aunty Belle's simple living illuminating the path I strive to follow. Like she did, I find happiness in each day's small events: feeding crumbs to birds in the garden or watching the colors of the Andes at dusk—pleasures accessible to the slow-moving and to those who pay close attention.

I hold up the second silver thimble. Simpler than the first, devoid of initials, its design is focused on functionality. It belonged to my grandmother Molly (Mary Aiken Wilson). She died when I was twelve, so my memories are vague. Her thimble speaks to me of a woman of strong character. Although I have a clear recollection of Molly's intervening on my behalf when my mother was scolding me, my mother insisted that my grandmother was very strict with her and her sister. Grandmother Molly must have passed on stringent standards for housekeeping as well, if my mother's own perfectionism in that regard is any indication. That Protestant work ethic must have a genetic component, one that I struggle to subdue. Women of my grandmother's and mother's generation sewed out of necessity. I learned to sew from my mother, making use of the thimbles she'd inherited. For many years, I enjoyed making my own clothes, but I was not nimble-fingered and lost interest and patience in wielding a needle, thimble, and thread when I began working full-time. I sold my Singer machine, which I'd shipped from the States. Santiago knows now not to ask me even to sew on a button for him.

Anyhow, I'd much prefer to spend my days in the garden, which conjures up remembrances of Grandmother Molly's fragrant roses anytime I sniff that flower. My mother also enjoyed digging in the soil. Happily, this family love of gardening also appears to be genetic. How barren life would be without my garden to tend.

The unusual coppery-bronze metal of the third thimble intrigues me. It seems a true expression of its owner, a progressive woman for her time. ASW: Anne Stenhouse Wilson. My grandmother Molly's sister, whom we called Aunta. Independent and strong-willed, she never married. Aunta graduated in the first nursing class of the University of California in 1917 and joined the army during the war, though, because of illness, she never went overseas. She took on private jobs, spending her life caring for others. Perhaps her example of compassion prompted my own interest in serving others as a Peace Corps volunteer and, later, as a teacher.

When Aunta was in her nineties and I in my twenties, I'd visit her on Sundays at Mrs. Thomas's Rest Home in Berkeley. Direct and outspoken in her opinions, she once chided that in my miniskirt I was "exhibiting myself to the whole world." Yet a wee crack appeared in her otherwise irreproachable conduct. I suspect her thimble found another use outside her sewing box. My mother discovered a bottle of sherry hidden in Aunta's closet. It seemed that Aunta, always a teetotaler, liked to imbibe a thimbleful of spirits.

My grandmother and great-aunts were staunch, staid Presbyterian Scotswomen, prim and proper, as were many women of their generation. My mother conserved a certain amount of that staidness, which naturally influenced my growing years. It's taken me a lifetime to peel off the layers of reserve, to be less responsible, to dare to go beach parasailing and to opt for a single kayak over the double one. Not that I'd go to the extreme of becoming a thimble-knocking lady of the night—women renowned for tapping their thimbles on a client's window to announce their arrival—but I'm glad I was around for Ray Charles, caffè lattes, Doris Lessing, and miniskirts.

That all three women immigrated to the United States in their youth speaks to an ability to face risk and adapt. I, also an immigrant, have drawn upon their legacy of strength.

The three thimbles adorn a glass shelf in my china cabinet. I worry, now that they have become mere decorations, that their voices will fall silent. I must make certain to pass them on to someone who will value these stories.

Wisteria

"They are nature, omnipotent, cruel, vast, and overwhelming. Awesome beauty, strange, tilted earth. You feel—when will it tilt again?" My mother wrote this description of the Andes in her journal while visiting us in Chile. Words I might have written.

Only in 2003, seven years after her death, did I summon the courage to open her two small diaries, untouched in a cubbyhole of my grandmother's desk. I battled the thought that to read them would be unethical, an invasion of her privacy, or that I'd find something I didn't want to know.

I was her only child, but we never developed a close relationship. Even now, the reasons remain nebulous. I can point to her negativity, her subtle put-downs, her workaholic drive, but I must accept some of the responsibility. I have few recollections of her laughing. She did not take criticism well, and I was afraid I'd hurt her if I told her what annoyed me. Looking back, I recognize my need as a young woman to put some distance between us. Once I left for the university, I began my journey of self-discovery in the diverse environment of Berkeley, free from her negativity, and each visit home felt suffocating. After graduation, I never considered returning to my small hometown. I'd studied international relations and Spanish, and now the world called to me. I spent the next two years in Colombia as a Peace Corps volunteer. Later, I moved to Chile to marry my boyfriend, Santiago, whom I'd met and fallen in love with while living in Berkeley.

After four decades, I continue to feel guilt about the sadness my decisions caused my parents. I've saved their letters, and, rereading them, I'm acutely reminded of their sorrow. We could afford to visit them only every two years with our boys. I hold a vivid scene in my memory of my mother and me standing in the kitchen. Recently arrived, I'm chattering, anxious to talk, share my Chilean life. But soon I feel myself closing up, like a poppy at sundown. Now I read a journal entry during one of her visits to Chile. She says of me, "She is a little warmer this time, but still no close talks. . . ."

It doesn't take me long to read through her few dozen journal pages. Mother wrote mainly when traveling or attending church retreats. Her love of the natural world is a thread woven throughout, and I'm shocked to realize how closely her words mirror my own thoughts. I feel both plagiarized and jealous of her ability to write.

After my father's death, she speaks of the mourning process and her loneliness. She reveals her low self-esteem in these pages and questions why she seems to have a talent for saying the wrong thing. I begin to realize how little I understood her.

At the age of eighty, she writes of an ancient wisteria vine, stooped and aged, its trunk wrinkled, dry, and pockmarked. How can it be alive? she asks. But, looking upward, she sees "graceful tender tendrils reaching out from wizened branches toward air, sun, and sky, testament to life still surging within." She says God is conveying a message: "Be strong as this wizened trunk. Have faith and grow." She yearns to remain an active, contributing member of her community but laments her deteriorating balance. "Too many unexplained falls, tipping over like an unbalanced doll." And, a year later: "Has my writing deteriorated, or what?" How I can empathize now as I approach the age she was when she wrote those words!

Her writing during church retreats reveals the joy and comfort she finds in that loving community of women. "So many special times and events during this gathering . . . lots of little miracles." Here, I get a glimpse into her growing spiritual life. She writes, "Much that was spiritual came from my aunts. As I grow older, I hope to be more like them. I pray to be and think maybe I am. At least, I am Presbyterian!"

This was quite a revelation to me, as I was raised Catholic, like my father, and my mother often attended Mass with us. It was after my father's death that she joined the Presbyterian church in town, obviously returning to her true comfort zone. I began accompanying her to her church services when I visited, meeting her newfound friends who were there for her when I wasn't.

Sometimes I wonder, if she were given a day back with the living and were sitting with me here now, whether we could overcome our entrenched barriers and talk. What would we say to each other? Could I move past my discomfort?

I certainly would thank her, recalling all the things she taught me to love: bird watching and camping, gardening and cooking, a good book, an uncluttered house, California Bears Saturday football games. I would tell her that she taught me to be independent and self-reliant.

I hope we'd laugh together, something we seldom did, except around my small boys. And I'd tell her that I wish she had loosened up! That I, too, have the tendency to be serious and intellectual, and that, like hers, my social skills sometimes fail me.

In her journal she wrote, "How I need to learn to listen and discern what others are really saying, thinking, and, especially, feeling." I wouldn't tell her that her habit of interrupting others and relating every topic of conversation back to herself irritated and embarrassed me. Instead, I might say that from her I learned to strive to be an attentive listener, while admitting that a major challenge in my life is giving an ear to my own inner needs and instincts.

Maybe she'd laugh if I said, "Remember the last pair of new shoes you bought, black with red and white soles? I wore them for years and only recently was able to part with them. And the white T-shirt with the hummingbird? It seemed to personify you, but I finally gave it away."

I think I know what she'd say to me. She wrote in her journal that my visits, which became more frequent as she aged, were the highlight of her year. "She is such a wonderful person. I'm so proud of her. She has made such a wonderful adjustment to living in another culture, raising two great kids, and keeping her marriage alive and well—not always easy, I know."

I'd confess my two greatest regrets: moving to another continent meant leaving her and my father alone, and not having been with her at the end.

On that November night when she died alone, thousands of miles to the north, it was I who felt abandoned. Why didn't she wait for me?

Soon after, the dream started. Always the same. My father and I are alone in our family home. My mother has gone away, and we don't know where or when she'll return. She didn't tell us. Not even a note. She does this more than once, and we're puzzled and hurt by this new behavior.

It is so unlike her.

Stepping Out

June 2016. We're traveling with a Chilean couple and, after a Baltic cruise, have arrived in Amsterdam. It is on this European soil that I've begun my transformation and emerge from my cocoon. It isn't a conscious decision to step out of my timid, Spanish-speaking persona and slip into my liberated, American, English-speaking personality; it just happens.

A Sunday morning. I'm relishing my transformation and am flying high with unfurled wings. Our little group decides to go to Mass in a church where the Dutch word *Katholieke* over the arched entrance identifies we're at the right place. Inside, a cloud of incense greets us. The small church is plain compared with the rich decoration of others we've visited. There's plenty of room, and we choose a pew near the front.

A man and a woman, both wearing priest's vestments, prepare to celebrate the Mass. I assume she is his assistant, maybe a deacon. The woman stands in the center behind the altar and begins the Mass singing a Gregorian chant. The man swings the incense burner and then takes a seat to the side. Surely, he will perform the consecration. The woman steps into the pulpit and preaches a lengthy sermon in Dutch. Parts of the Mass follow a slightly different sequence than that to which we are accustomed. When it is time for the greeting of peace, I turn to the worshipers behind me, shake their hands, and murmur, "Peace be with you" in English. The woman then sings the consecration as a Gregorian chant. The man is clearly the "assistant." I am of an ecumenical, open-minded bent and have no objection to women priests, but I'm confused. As far as I know, Rome has yet to give them the go-ahead. Was there a Vatican Council I missed? Santiago and our friends must be completely bewildered. But we are here, and "when in Rome . . ." I rise and follow the worshipers up to the communion rail. My companions trail behind me.

We cross ourselves as the woman priest gives the final blessing. Turning to leave, I see that the man behind is looking at me. We smile.

He asks in English, "Where are you from?"

"We live in Chile," I tell him, "but I'm American."

"Were you confused by this?" he asks.

"Well, yes! A woman priest?"

"This is an old Catholic church of the Netherlands," he explains. "Centuries ago, part of the Dutch Catholic Church split off from the Roman Catholics. We don't recognize the infallibility of the pope or the Immaculate Conception. There are few of these churches now. As you can see, our congregation is small."

"That's interesting. I had no idea!"

"Several years ago, we began accepting women as priests, and our priests can marry. We also accept divorce. Would you like to join us in another room for coffee?"

"Thank you. I'll check with my friends."

But my travel companions have already made their exit. I stop to chat with the woman priest, who is happy to inform this perplexed Catholic about her church. She repeats the invitation for coffee, but I tell her that we have plans to go out of town and cannot accept. I worry that she might have felt slighted.

Madrid. Two days later. It is hot and humid. We've stopped at an outdoor café across the street from the cathedral for a cool drink. I notice a pile of rags at the foot of a traffic signal. The pile moves. It's an old woman. I wonder why she is sitting in the searing sun and resolve to give her a few coins before we leave. But then she rises, retrieves an old pair of sandals from behind a low wall, puts them on, and shuffles past.

I stand. "I want to give something to that woman," I say, and run after her. "Señora!"

She stops, and I hand her the coins. We look at each other and smile. I return to my chair, whereupon the woman next to us goes after the old lady and also hands her some coins. Then, back at her table, she picks up a piece of sandwich from her plate and takes it to the woman.

That same day, we stop to cool off at another outdoor café. A tall, very pregnant African woman attired in her native dress circulates among the tables. My first reaction, and that of the others, is to pretend not to notice her. But again I am curious— about the necklaces she carries in her hand and, yes, about her story. She sees me looking and stops at our table.

I ask, "*De que son?* What are they made of?"

"Coconut shell," she replies in accented Spanish.

"Where are you from?" I just have to ask. The others probably want to kick me under the table.

"Senegal."

"And how long have you been in Spain?"

"Seven months."

She holds out the necklaces to me.

"No, gracias." I smile and shake my head, but I give her a coin. She hands me a tiny elephant bead.

"*Regalo.* A gift. For you," she says, and moves on, holding out the necklaces to the diners at the next table.

El Mercado de San Miguel teems with summer tourists. So many tempting goodies to eat but nowhere to sit. Santiago and I each buy a slice of pizza and wander to look for an empty seat.

Someone grabs my arm from behind. A tall, blue-eyed, blond woman gestures to me to take the barstool where she has been sitting. In front of her stands a glass of champagne. I thank her and sit to eat my pizza quickly, while Santiago stands next to me at the bar. The woman remains by my side.

She hasn't said a word, so I ask, "Where are you from?"

She smiles slightly and gazes off into the distance, her head held high. "From Jordan."

"Jordan? You don't look Jordanian."

Again she smiles—a secretive smile. After a pause, she says, "No, I'm kidding. I lived there for a while. The people there are dark. The men are very, very dark. Negro, black." She points to her head. "Dark here, too."

Of course I wonder what she was doing in Jordan. I picture her following an exotic lover, later to be heartbroken.

"I am from Russia, near the Urals," she says.

Well, that makes more sense.

"And now?"

"I live in northern Spain."

I hesitate slightly before asking her, "What do you do there?"

She smiles. "I make money. *Mucho dinero.*"

She sips her champagne. Her glassy gaze tells me she's had several before this one. Then she leans in to me, lifts up the hair covering my ear, and whispers confidences. She has been disappointed in love, she tells me. Her eyes turn moist.

I want to be sympathetic. Why did she grab *my* arm? Maybe she sees a mother figure in this white-haired lady. "What's your name?" I ask.

"Gina."

"I'm Suzanne."

She lifts my hair like a curtain and leans in to my ear again. Her low, slurred words do nothing to clarify more of this mysterious woman.

Our pizzas long finished, I say we have to go. Gina circles me with her arms, and we hug. Her last words are "Pray for me."

"I will."

I do. And I see the tiny elephant bead on my night table and wonder how the Senegalese woman and her baby are and whether the beggar woman has a place to sleep at night.

Intermittent Friendships

I receive an email from my friend Laura, who left Chile with her four children twenty years ago and who announces that she and her daughters are coming here for a funeral and need a place to stay. We have plenty of room, I tell her. Since her last visit, thirteen years ago, we've been in touch only sporadically, our lives seemingly full and complete with family and work. What fun it will be to catch up after all this time.

When they arrive, Laura and I hug and laugh. She must reintroduce me to her daughters, whom I knew only as children and who are now grown women. The girls' father lives here, and they spend time visiting with him and his side of the family. Laura and I set up dates to meet for dinner, lunch, coffee with other friends from the past, all Americans married to Chileans, and who figured we'd always be here. It's a time for reminiscing about the days when our children played together. We wonder, "Whatever happened to . . . ? Do you keep in touch with . . . ?" We arrived in Chile at a time of social and economic turmoil. Oil, meat, basic necessities were in short supply. Protests, terrorist bombs, nighttime curfews were our daily bread. But we were resilient and prevailed in spite of a coup d'état and eighteen years of military dictatorship. Laura and I met at a Lamaze class while expecting our first children in 1974. Doctors and relatives were puzzled by our preference for natural childbirth.

Expat friendships, formed on foreign soil, are particularly vulnerable. Some friends returned to the States. Some divorced or were widowed; others went in search of better economic opportunities. Some of us are still here decades later, having sometimes drifted apart when children attended different schools or when we settled in different neighborhoods or work left us little time to socialize.

Seated with two of our old gringa group, I am struck by the wonder of this encounter. "Look at us—gray-haired grand-mothers now! Did we ever imagine back then that decades later we'd be sitting around, remembering the days when we were young and energetic and hopeful for the future?"

What impresses me is how quickly and easily we reconnect. The basis for friendship is still there. We feel the sorrow of a mother for her deceased child and sympathize with another over the difficulties of dealing long-distance with an ailing, aging mother.

"Let's start up our group again! Maybe for birthdays?" I suggest.

Another day, four of us, including Laura, meet for lunch. More laughter and questions. We ask about the children we knew as toddlers and now want reassurance that they are doing well. We update each other on our jobs and families and share photos, names, and ages of grandchildren.

Laura is the center of attention.

"I remember the cookies you were always making!"

"My Nicholas remembers your old house and the big apri-cot tree in your backyard."

"It's really amazing how we can seem to pick up the threads from when we were last all together."

Laura's eyes turn watery. "It's because we lived through some emotional times with each other."

Laura has gone. The house feels empty. She texts when she arrives in Texas: the trip went well, and her heart is full.

Although she came for a funeral, she received an unexpected gift: the opportunity to reconnect with old friends.

Her visit sheds blessings on me as well. I'd let some friendships lapse. Yet this is the stage in life when time is my frequent companion. Writing at the keyboard and cutting dead flowers don't completely fulfill me. I resolve to nurture these renewed friendships. A round from my Girl Scout days comes to mind:

Make new friends, but keep the old;
One is silver, the other gold.

I open my address book and update phone numbers and addresses. Laura and I are now connected via WhatsApp.

VIII. GOING GRAY

Unlike many of our forebears, we, the children of the Age of Aquarius, were allowed to be seen and heard as children. Now in our seventh and eighth decades, we continue to make our voices heard. We are determined to remain visible and relevant while facing new challenges: the need for compassion as we care for aging parents, and resilience as we face our own health issues. Life lessons and growing awareness that our time on this planet is limited influence the decisions we make and the way we want to spend our days.

On Turning Seventy

As an irrigator guides water to the fields, as an archer aims an arrow, as a carpenter carves wood, the wise shape their lives.
                                                            —The Buddha

"I've decided to go gray," I told Andrés, my hairdresser. "Can you do something to make the process less frightful? Like a rinse and maybe a more modern cut?" I pointed to a hairstyle in a glossy magazine. I hoped he knew of a magical way to let my gray see the light of day after decades of a camouflaging dye. Until now, I had lacked the courage for this move, especially in Chile, where 99.9 percent of women dye their hair well into their nineties.

In past months, the idea that my seventieth birthday was approaching was much on my mind. Me. Seventy. But now, as I pass that milestone, I find myself looking forward to this new decade, despite body changes that I observe with curiosity: turkey-wattle neck, bat-wing underarms, chin hairs that sprout overnight, and, most troubling, sagging facial muscles resulting in a sourpuss expression. I make conscious efforts to smile to avoid others' thinking I'm angry. I curse as I struggle to open a jar of olives. In bed, give me a good book. But there are some advantages: no more shaving legs, no more sanitary pads, senior rates at the theater. And now, no more dyeing. Seventy feels like the right moment to let nature have her way with my hair.

With the perspective of years, I've come to see gray as representing wisdom, kindness, and forgiveness, a woman capable of releasing grudges and envy like balloons into the sky. I consider my graying locks a symbol of pride in my age, a declaration. *Yes! I'm an older (mind you, not yet elderly) woman.*

My newfound confidence wavers when I confront my image in a storefront window. A voice inside me suggests that there's a hint of narcissism in this process. Am I simply changing the image I want to project? Another voice counters that accepting the gray is really an act of humility.

Inner transformations accompany the growing wrinkles and sags. I've learned more about myself—a self that, despite physical aging and memory lapses, still has the potential to flourish with the passage of time.

My values and priorities are more clearly defined. I seek what Anne Morrow Lindbergh in her *Gift from the Sea* refers to as the "simplification of life," a way of living "conducive to inner and outer harmony." I resist new acquisitions that encumber me. Yes, if our thirty-year-old refrigerator dies, I know we'll need a new one. But I take pleasure in using the familiar Christmas decorations again and again. I love finding new homes for things no longer needed: my best black pants that I can barely button, the dainty copper sandals that slide off my feet, white linen tablecloths I hate to iron. How light I feel now that those things are gone.

I welcome new books or plants for my garden. But *please* don't give me more serving dishes, cookbooks, place mats, necklaces, or vases. For my birthday, my husband gave me my first laptop, a wonderful portable acquisition, an excellent upgrade from my aging desktop.

Lindbergh speaks of women's need for times of solitude to achieve grace and harmony. Time is the precious gift of this age that I treasure and hope to use wisely: to observe a bumblebee at my solanum flowers, to walk in the park, to read a poem, to make today a little better than yesterday. When the cleaning lady wants to talk about her medical problems, I listen and help her decipher the doctor's prescription and suggest that she follow his orders and eat less bread.

Now a news junkie, I start my days checking the morning newspaper. In the science section, a telescopic photograph of a star in formation has me pondering the vast unknowns of the universe. I read of a new species of frog and of progress in the treatment for ALS, which took my father's life.

At seventy, I welcome hearty, out-loud laughter, whether it be at email jokes, granddaughter-tickling bouts, or Speedy Gonzalez as he sneaks into our bedroom. And at day's end, I think back to instances that brought me joy: a son's phone call, a clear blue sky, the bright purple of the jacaranda, the smile of a stranger walking her dog.

The new cut pleases me. Shorter, tousled. I look around for other female gray heads for moral support. When we cross paths, we look at each other and smile, as if we possess some secret. Yet they are few—my silver tresses make me stand out in a crowd.

I rather like that.

Swift as the Wild Goose Flies

The words in the newspaper jump out at me: "All ages. No experience required." Does that include a seventy-year-old woman with stiff joints?

I've always wanted to try kayaking. It suggests adventure and an intimate way to dip my senses into the natural world. I'm long past walking the Pacific Crest Trail, but kayaking? Why not?

I read on. It would be a guided trip across Tomales Bay in Northern California, all equipment provided. Such an expedition requires courage. I need company, so I propose the idea to Martha and Jack, the friends I'm staying with during my visit back to my hometown. To my delight, they agree.

Early Saturday morning in a veil of fog, we wind along California's Highway One bordering the coast of the bay. Past the town of Marshall, we locate the small boat harbor alongside Nick's Cove, where we meet up with Brett, our young guide. For the next half hour, he patiently explains the gear we'll be wearing: an awkward blue plastic spray skirt hung from suspenders, to be topped by an orange life jacket. He demonstrates how to hold and swing the paddle, how to place our legs, and how to stretch the elasticized rim of the skirt around the kayak's opening. This is going to be more complicated than I expected.

Before us are three kayaks: a needle-thin blue one for Brett, a double and a single one for us.

"Who wants to go in the single?" asks Brett.

I raise my hand. No wimpy double kayaks for me.

The morning mist begins to lift, and the bay waters shimmer, smooth as liquid silver, before us. Like ducklings, we follow Brett northwest toward our destination, a small beach on a peninsula at the opposite shore, home to a herd of tule elk. Farther out, the wind begins to ruffle the bay waters. I slow to view a scattering of ducks and then paddle wildly to catch up with the others. We skim past the tops of oyster beds dotted with scurrying sanderlings that pay no heed to our intrusion.

The farther out into the bay we advance, the stronger whips the wind—and the harder I must exert my sagging biceps. From the corner of my eye, I spot something in the water following me. I turn. Nothing there. Paddle. Right. Left. Right. Left. I turn again. There it is. Big, winsome eyes staring out from a silky, round head. A harbor seal. "Hi there," I call. "Are you spying on me?" The seal plays hide-and-seek until I reach the beach.

Brett yanks our kayaks onto the sand. I wonder how I'll extract myself from my vessel and unfold my cramped legs, but it's surprising what one can do when one's pride is at stake. Finally, in upright position, I wobble toward the table Brett has set up with snacks of local cheese, bread, and strawberries as he explains that the varying vegetation on the bay's opposing sides is due to a fault line running under it.

Needing to stretch my legs, I follow Jack up a nearby hill, where we sight two tule elk. Then, back on the beach, we don our gear for the return.

"Who wants to try the single kayak on the way back?" I ask.

Martha volunteers. I settle into the double one in front of Jack, and we start off. Wow. Sharing the work is a gentle breeze.

Then Martha calls, "I don't feel very stable. I'd like to change back." Returning to shore, I once more angle my body into the single kayak.

Brett announces, "We'll have the wind in our favor, but the tide's against us."

It feels like everything is against us. Brett calls to me, "Try using the rudder." Working the alternating pedals makes the job easier, but Nick's Cove is just a tiny speck in the distance that isn't getting any bigger. Twist left. Paddle. Pull. Twist right. Paddle. Pull. My sleeves are wet, and I taste salt water in my mouth, but this is what I came for—a challenge and intimacy with this bay on whose shores I splashed as a child, screaming at the sight of transparent jellyfish.

Left paddle. Right paddle. Will the shore ever get closer? I imagine a bowl of hot clam chowder waiting for me at Nick's Cove and push onward, singing aloud an old Girl Scout song: *Our paddles clean and bright, flashing like silver, swift as the wild goose flies. Dip, dip, and swing. Dip, dip, and swing.*

At last. The dock. The tip of my kayak glides onto the ramp where Brett waits. I want to punch my fist into the air with a jubilant "Yes!" I've proven to myself that I'm capable of a demanding physical feat, after years of being overshadowed by my super-athlete husband and sons. Oh, I know I'll never become a Pam Houston, braving the white waters of a wild Colorado River, but I will and can do this again.

Never has clam chowder tasted so good.

Me, Myself, and Memory

A former Peace Corps colleague sent me a photo of a group of us on the beach in Cartagena, Colombia. There's no doubt that the young, thin woman stretched out on the sand is I. But I have no recollection of that day trip fifty years ago. It's as if I lost that day of my life.

So many moments, days, people, and events have vanished in the convoluted folds of my cerebral cortex. My eldest son, Danny, mentioned that I took him to the doctor several times as a child for his back ailments. I felt miserable because I didn't remember. I thought it was his brother, Nico, who had the back problems. I've always believed that our memories are selective, recalling significant people and events in our lives. Yet this was my own son whose medical history I'd forgotten. When I say, "I don't remember," do my sons think, *She's losing it?*

Neurologist Oliver Sacks said that it is memory that makes our lives. This starts me thinking: what things *do* I remember? The list of visual scenes is endless: my family home, the floor plan of a grandmother's house, the springer spaniel we had when I was a child, the face of my father taking his last breaths, Danny standing on the toilet while I dried his hair with the hair dryer, the night I met my husband. Remembered smells (the dry summer grasses of California hills, pungent redwood groves, Coppertone suntan lotion, my husband's pajamas) and sounds (the whistle of a train, rain on the roof, a voice on the telephone) often trigger visual images. My memory is particularly sharp at recalling the many times I've put my foot in my mouth.

Yet, as I age, memory lapses multiply like aphids on my

roses in spring. Frustrating, though not life-threatening, is my difficulty recalling names of actors and singers. One in particular gives me trouble time and time again, so I've trained myself to remember the letter *O*. Then the name comes to me. Oh, yes! Olivia Newton-John. Sometimes I must go through the entire alphabet until I recall the name of the woman across the room.

Word retrieval is tricky when two languages are involved. I'll be speaking in Spanish when a key word comes to me only in English, or vice versa. This is especially stressful when I'm in the company of several people. I turn to my husband for help. "What's the word in Spanish for . . . ? That thing that . . . You know . . ." But he doesn't know what the devil I'm referring to.

For my experiential recollections, my imagination must fill in the gaping holes, allowing me to shape the memory to my own liking. This can lead to disagreement when I'm remembering a shared event with someone: "But it wasn't like that at all!"

Another type of exchange not unusual in our household goes like this:

"I did tell you!"

"No, you did not!"

"Yes, I did. I distinctly remember. We were standing in the kitchen." At this point, I give up. Who's to say whose memory is more accurate? (Though I continue to be convinced I'm right.)

I envy those who have been constant in keeping journals over the years. I'm a sporadic journalist, though when traveling, I do take a pencil and notebook along.

I recently came across a forgotten diary I'd kept during a visit to Colombia. Rereading it was a revelation and a joy that brought back lost moments, details, and impressions: the rocky, wild bus ride into the barrio, a small mulatta girl asking me if I was an albino, the death of my friend Ana, a trip with eight-year-old Hansi for his first view of the ocean.

Although I lament and wonder about the many forgotten moments—books I've read, children I taught, dances I danced—I believe that they have stayed with me. I *am* my memories—whether remembered, forgotten, or in progress.

Sins of Omission

I'm sitting with my mother-in-law for a while this morning, rubbing her thin hand—the one not connected to the tube—and smoothing wisps of white hair off her forehead. One hundred and three years of age, Señora Olga has stopped eating and drinking.

I help the nurse bathe her, gently turning her whisper of a body, naked upon the sheets, bereft of any modesty. What I see in that spent woman, who bore five children and mended the socks of eleven grandchildren, is a life fulfilled, although in recent years, committing to memory the names of her twenty-two great-grandchildren became too great a task for her.

In my own family, we were ill at ease with our bodies, disinclined to express our feelings physically. Hugs were stiff and awkward. Coming of age in the 1960s, the touchy-feely era, I grew comfortable hugging friends and, of course, boyfriends, but that ease did not extend to family, and even less to aging grandparents and great-aunts. Years later, I felt I overcame a barrier when I first rubbed my eighty-year-old mother's swollen legs with body lotion and trimmed the toenails she could no longer reach. I wish I'd been more generous. Once she was widowed—maybe even before—she might have longed for me, her only child, to give her more than an occasional squeeze.

Her three-year stay at a facility for seniors allowed me frequent contact with the residents. There, I discovered how easy it was to bring smiles to their faces—Sadie, Norma, Bertha—by engaging them in conversation and listening to their stories, revealing to me my underdeveloped potential for giving.

When my grown sons come to visit, I hold them close, not

too proud to say, "Come on. Give me a good hug." But I do wish I didn't have to ask for it. Perhaps this is one of the lessons we're meant to pass on to the younger generations.

According to her children, Señora Olga was not a physically affectionate mother, but in the past year she's begun seeking more physical contact. During recent visits, she's rubbed my hands and lifted her face for a kiss. Now she is giving me another opportunity to redeem myself.

Today, sitting next to her bed, I watch the rise and fall of her frail chest as she draws labored breaths and give her what I sense she wants, though she can no longer express it. I stroke her hand in gratitude for helping me past my aversion to an aging, sagging body and allowing me to witness these intimate moments of taking leave of the living world of comforting touch.

The Trail of Torture

*Of all the paths you take in life, make sure a few of them are
dirt.*
                                                    —John Muir

The sign reads LAGO LEONES: 5.5 MILES. One way. One of our
guides says, "It's relatively flat most of the way." I wonder what
"most of the way" means.

Spectacular mountain ridges border the valley. Gleaming
glaciers hug several peaks, the sky a clear blue, and I take several deep breaths of the fresh Patagonian air. Two guides, Pablo
and Sebastián, lead our group of five hikers of varying ages and
states of physical fitness. A husband-wife team carries ski poles,
though he wears blue jeans, as if he has a short jaunt in mind.
She is tall and thin, and her hiking attire screams, *I'm experienced.*
She wears a floppy hat with a back flap to prevent neck sunburn,
a breathable fabric blouse, heavy-duty pants, and boots topped
with gaiters. Her girlfriend, in casual outdoor wear, looks less
fit. Santiago, a lifelong athlete, is in good shape. And me? Well,
I tell myself, I *do* exercise regularly, though it's been a year since
I last wore my hiking boots. Pablo did say the terrain is mostly
flat, so no ski poles for me. I like to have my hands free as I walk
and carry a simple backpack with water and lunch.

As we start off through a plantation of young pines, the husband-wife team takes off like a shot—just behind Pablo. Soon,
all I see are their backsides in the distance. *What are they trying to
prove? Is this a race? What about enjoying nature?* The group strings
out into a single line; the other guide, Sebastián, covers the
rear—which is me. Santiago hangs back with me—for a while.

"What's the matter?" he asks. "The others are way ahead."

"Something in my shoe is rubbing against my foot. I need to stop to check it out." I don't want to remind him of my arthritis or my lazy foot, a consequence of old back surgery. Also, I prefer not to pay much attention to these physical ailments or admit to myself that my age is slowing me down.

Pablo didn't mention that we'd be crossing rivulets of glacier melts, balancing on branches and wobbly wooden slat bridges, or that the "flat" nevertheless ascends into steep, forested slopes of narrow, rocky ledges studded with protruding tree roots. I cling to a rope to clamber along a slanted, wide rock face. A rickety wooden ladder facilitates a tricky vertical descent. Through the trees, I spot the rushing, milky-green Leones River. Now it's just fresh-out-of-college Sebastián and I. I thank him over and over for his steady, helping hands and apologize that he's stuck with me. I feel like an aging mountain goat, abandoned by the herd.

Pablo checks with Sebastián by radio. "How is she doing? Tell her to keep in mind the return trek."

Believe me, I know.

"How much farther?" I ask Sebastián. "I don't want to give up, but I'm worried I'll slow the others down."

"About two more miles. See that hill ahead? The lake is over that rise."

"That's it," I tell him. "Let's stop here." We devour our lunches in a small wood. I remove my shoes—ah, what relief—and peel off my socks to find a raw, red blister on the side of my foot. I lie back in prickly shrubbery to rest and gaze up at the trees. I'm in paradise but too damn tired to care.

Soon—too soon—Sebastián stands. "We'd better start back."

The return trek is interminable. I'm aware only of the blister. I shuffle, one foot in front of the other, skirting rocks, fording streamlets, my boots sinking into grassy tufts sprouting from muddy islets. I don't have the strength to climb the stairs onto the wooden slat bridge. Feeling old and decrepit, I grab Sebastián's outstretched hand. On the other side, we stop to fill our water bottles with glacial water, and I dip my tender feet into the icy rivulet.

We enter the pine plantation, the last stretch. When will it end? This seems much longer than when we started out. I mutter under my breath. *Damn trees.* But then—there's the meadow ahead. We cross another stream, hopping from rock to rock. A blue-and-white kingfisher observes us from a nearby branch.

"Look, Sebastián." I point. "A martin pescador!"

He turns for a look and then points ahead. "There's the truck."

With the last of my strength, I hobble to it, haul myself into the passenger seat, lay my head back, and close my eyes.

Was it worth it?

If I'm honest, no. I hate to admit it to myself, even less to the others, but I did not enjoy the hike. My immediate thought is, *I need to get into better shape.* But then I realize that what matters is that I'm able to accept my limitations. I know when it's time to call it quits, and I'm all right with my decision.

The others come crawling up to the truck thirty minutes later. I listen to their glowing descriptions of the panorama I'll never see in real life. Fortunately, they'll show me their photos later and I'll imagine myself being there.

IX. BIRDS OF A FEATHER

A defining characteristic of every landscape I've ever loved is its birdsong. When I return to my hometown, I step outside to inhale the scent of its particular vegetation and listen to the birds: the raucous calls of the shiny ebony crows, the two-note call of the towhee (tow-hee, tow-hee), *the boisterous* waka-waka-waka *of the woodpecker. It is then I know I'm truly back home. During my Patagonian travels, I've incorporated into my birdsong repertoire the distinctive calls of the ibis, the kingfisher, and the* chucao tapaculo. *In my city backyard, the melodies of the yellow finches, the trill of the tufted tit-tyrants and* rat-a-tat *of the rufous-tailed plant cutter are music to my ears. Listening to their songs is one of the great, small pleasures of my days.*

Santiago's Green Dilemma

I heard them before I saw them. From the upper limbs of the towering araucaria tree came a strident clamor. There. In the tree's prickly top notch. A blob of intertwining branches, like a giant, roughly woven basket. From several holes peered green-and-gray heads with beady eyes. I tipped my head back to better see the parrot condo.

In the forests of southern Chile I've often seen the emerald flocks of the *choroy* parrot. But parrots in Santiago, Chile's capital? This was a first. A closer look revealed they were not the native *choroy*. These were invaders. Identified as Argentine *cotorras* (*Myiopsitta monachus*), in English they're known as Quaker or monk parrots. Locals speculated. How did they get here? Surely not by flying over the Andes from Argentina. Perhaps offspring of escaped pets?

When first sighted more than twenty years ago, they limited their habitat to the trees of a golf course and a neighboring ham radio antenna. Now, flocks of the gregarious marauders fly over my house every morning on the lookout for breakfast. They've discovered the plump persimmons on my neighbor's tree, once the sole domain of austral thrushes. They snack on the seeds of the round, prickly liquidambar pods, where, other years, wild canaries performed acrobatics as they foraged for seeds. I've seen the parrots waddling across the grass of city parks. Reproducing at a rapid rate, when things get too crowded, they seek another tree, preferably a conifer, to install a new condo. Urban parrot sprawl or an immigrant seeking out an ecological niche?

Santiago is not the only parrot city. On Saturdays in New

York City you can join a Brooklyn wild-parrot safari to observe Quaker parrots, supposedly escapees from a shipment from Argentina.

In some places, the little green-and-gray parrot is considered an outlaw, but how do you outlaw a parrot, or any bird, for that matter? It's the old story of the farmers versus the birders. The parrots are cute and sociable, but, say the detractors, they eat rice, corn, and sunflower crops and decimate the indigenous birds' food supply.

The Quaker parrot population has stabilized in New York City. Not so in Santiago. I have no doubt that they are "easy breeders." Though it's impossible to calculate their growing numbers, I did count eighteen of them one winter morning, gorging themselves on the liquidambar seed pods next door. They have no natural predators, although our neighbor's gray cat was making a valiant effort to claw its way up the liquidambar. But the clever parrots took off in a green flash of chatter that sounded a lot like laughter.

Dire warnings that the parrots will displace the native bird population and that the huge nests will eventually kill the host trees sound a lot like the ongoing human drama as waves of "nonnative" immigrants and refugees—ethnically and culturally different from the locals—pour into more developed countries. Locals worry about how their country and their lives will be impacted. How will these newcomers adapt and manage to satisfy their needs? Of course, this dilemma is way more serious than the parrot issue, for it involves human lives. And we, if we are caring, compassionate humans, can affect outcomes. We just might benefit from observing how the birds adapt to newcomers. Perhaps "adapt" is the key word for all the actors involved, as, throughout the long history of this extraordinary planet, all living things have always had to make accommodations for changing habitat and new neighbors.

As an observer of this unfolding bird drama, I wonder about the uncertain future of the petite wild canaries, whose flutelike chatter and dainty ways contrast starkly with the bold, noisy presence of the green Johnny come-latelys. Yet, I've noticed how the austral thrushes take turns with the parrots at the persimmon tree and how the neighborhood canaries feed on other trees adjacent to the parrots' preferred liquidambar.

This gives me hope that the newcomers and the old-timers, avian and human, will work it out.

I'll be watching.

Patagonian Punk

All morning, Santiago and I trekked with our friends up and down rocky slopes, along ravines and across heath lands, invigorated by the rushing of glacial streams and curiosity for the sights we'd find around the next bend. Despite heat, dust, and aching feet, our spirits were high when we finally reached Camp Poincenot, far from crowds and cars, billboards and Internet. Here it was just us, like-minded hikers, and the splendor of the natural world. We stood breathless below the bare, vertical spires of Mt. Fitzroy and its surrounding peaks, a glacier-ringed massif straddling a contested stretch of border between Argentina and Chile. Just beyond lay the formidable, mysterious Patagonian southern ice cap.

As we headed back down the mountainside, only one thing was lacking: a glimpse of the rare, giant Magellanic woodpecker. We'd passed through cool pockets of ancient beech woods, eyes peeled for a flash of bright red and ears perked for the giveaway *toc-toc*, but to no avail.

But then Santiago halted. In a clearing, a man was aiming the telescopic lens of his camera toward the upper trunk of a tree, snapping photos from different angles. Our bird-watchers' radar switched to high alert. Signaling to our companions to follow, we moved off the trail for a closer look, quietly slipping binoculars from backpacks.

"Woodpecker," the photographer whispered in a French accent.

Guided by the persistent drumming, I finally spotted it: nature's carpenter, a splash of scarlet atop ebony plumes.

A passing hiker, noticing our upward gazes, came over. *"Qué pasa?"*

"Carpintero," I whispered, and passed her my binoculars.

From the trail, loud voices, speaking German, broke the silence. We all turned, fingers to mouths, and *shh*-ed in unison. It was a couple with two children. They stopped to watch.

The woodpecker flapped noisily to another tree, closer to the trail. We all tiptoed after him. The bird's laughing cackle pierced the stillness. An answer rang out from a nearby tree. Scanning with sharpened senses, we sighted the punk, red-crested heads of three males and a black female, well-camouflaged in the shadows of a tree trunk. Our gawking and pointing and flashing of cameras in no way interrupted woodpecker mealtime. Heads bobbing, beaks jabbing, they worked the trees within a few feet of their audience, now a growing knot in the middle of the path.

Whispers in Italian, French, English, German, and Spanish danced in the silent woods. As hikers, we were drawn to these remote places to experience the peace afforded by forest, stream, and cathedral spires, as well as the thrill of a challenging climb. And, no doubt, the trail would have a surprise or two in store. Unexpectedly, we'd become a United Nations of hikers brought together by a family of woodpeckers. Gathered on the long-disputed border that afternoon, we spoke a common language: the language of wonder.

A Light Touch

As I walk the long beach under patchy morning fog, my senses are open, alert, receptive to the rhythmic plunging of the waves, the wind's feathery touch on my face, the scent of the salty sea. And yes! There are the Franklin gulls, recently arrived from their journey from the Northern Hemisphere, in their black-and-white summer plumage. They surge up to the receding wavelets and dart into the shallows, plucking morsels to their liking. They likely worked up a hearty appetite on their migration south. Sharing the shore with the gulls are several brown curlews, which take off and cry in alarm when I get too close. A pair of black-and-white, orange-beaked oyster catchers mingles with the shoreline avian gathering.

This beach has few shells or pebbles for the beachcomber. Clumps of tangled brown seaweed are strewn about, like abandoned tresses of sea sirens. What I notice are the interweaving prints in the sand: the deep tread marks of an outlaw jeep, imprints from shoe soles, dog pawprints, and the faint, dainty, three-toed patterns of the shorebirds.

While residing in northern climes, Franklin gulls construct their floating aquatic nests from vegetal materials on hand, while their diet helps reduce the population of pesky insects, garbage, and mice. These handsome, agile fellows molt twice a year. Two outfits a year. How lightly they tread this earth.

Back in the capital, my attention switches from seagulls to Speedy Gonzalez. Out of hibernation for more than a month, he's not his usual tortoise self: he's eating very little and squeezing into small places between flower pots to sleep. Could he just be getting old? I take him in a box to see a vet specialist in exotic animals. Speedy paces around the box, looking for escape.

Dr. Harrison informs me that Speedy is a *Chelonoidis chilensis* and weighs a kilo and a half. The vet explains that, in spite of its name, this type of tortoise comes from Argentina.

"How old is he?" he asks.

"We bought him over thirty years ago, a present for my son's sixth birthday," I say.

The vet examines Speedy's shell and checks inside his mouth. He suspects a respiratory problem but needs to do an X-ray to make a definite diagnosis. A tortoise X-ray? The only vet hospital with the required machine is in a netherworld south of downtown, somewhere I've never been. Great. Meanwhile, we must start him on antibiotics. The doctor demonstrates how to administer the drops to Speedy with a syringe, holding on to his neck and prying open his mouth. Okay. I can do that.

But it is clearly a two-person job, so I ask our cleaning lady to help. "I'll grab his neck and open his mouth, and you drop in the medicine." Every time I attempt to grab his head/neck, he whisks back into his shell. Finally, after a tug-of-war between Speedy and me, I manage to force open his tiny jaw and deliver the drops. I call the doc. "This is a real struggle."

"Try relaxing him, petting him." A gentler touch is needed.

The next day, I lift Speedy onto my lap, talk to him, and tickle his back legs. My lap is not where he wants to be, and, in his efforts to escape, out come his head and neck. Quick as a flash, I grasp his soft, squiggly neck skin. He resists. I insist, sticking the fingernail of my other hand into his jaw.

But after a few weeks, he hasn't gained weight and we must administer turtle mush to him as well. This requires patience; Speedy is a slow eater.

From what I can understand from the X-ray report, he has pneumonia. Now, after several days, he and I have gotten the knack of this medical ordeal. Though he has the strength of an ox, he is a gentle creature and has earned my respect. Like the Franklin gull, he treads this earth lightly.

Today I saw him eating grass. Good boy, Speedy!

Man treads the earth heavily, covering immense swaths with concrete, buildings, malls, trucks, dams, cars, and parking lots in which to leave the cars when not in use. We fill our lives with stuff: doodads, what-me-knots, bric-a-brac, short-life-span appliances, disposable water bottles, napkins, cell phones, and cameras. Disturbing the land is called progress.

Yet notice the lowly earthworm, that gentle aerator of soil; the pollinator butterfly and bee; the aphid-predator ladybug whose legs tickle my cupped hand; the unappreciated bat, terminator of gnats and mosquitoes; and Franklin's gulls, pirouetting at the shoreline. Quiet lessons for us to live lightly on this earth, taking only what we need, leaving soft footprints on the landscape during our brief passage through this wondrous planet.

St. Francis's Garden

It was probably the hottest day of the year—over ninety degrees and definitely hotter at four o'clock in the afternoon along the sizzling sidewalk of the Alameda, downtown Santiago's main artery. I had considered postponing my appointment, but no, Franciscan brother Jaime and I had each reconfirmed twice that we'd meet at this hour at the museum of the seventeenth-century San Francisco church.

Inside the museum's thick adobe walls, hung with large colonial religious paintings, it was dark and wonderfully cool. Why did colonial artists paint their scenes in such lugubrious colors? To instill the wrath of God in the illiterate faithful, I once heard. A young guide directed me to Brother Jaime's office in a corridor bordering a central garden, where he met me at the door with the traditional Chilean peck on the cheek, though we hadn't met before. I had expected him to be clad in the brown Franciscan habit, in keeping with the ancient walls around him; instead, he met me in T-shirt, chinos, and sandals. He led me to a table, where he sat at his laptop. The walls around us were lined with bookshelves, paintings, and a couple of Christmas stockings.

"Are you satisfied with the contract?" he asked.

I said it was fine, pulling out my copy, which conceded to me the rights to quote in my upcoming memoir some words of Gabriela Mistral, Chile's Nobel poetess. In her will, Gabriela left the rights to her work and all her property to Chile's Franciscan congregation.

We each signed our copies. Just then, a strident squawk sounded outside.

"Was that a peacock?"

Brother Jaime smiled. "Yes, the peahen is perched on some eggs. We also have exotic chickens and a pond with fish and a turtle. Down the hall is a small room dedicated to Gabriela, and you can see her Nobel medal."

I thanked him and said I thought I'd go enjoy the garden for a while.

Outside, tall, old trees provided welcome shade. A gnarled cork tree looked to have been planted there by the original monks. There was the peacock, an elegant queen on her ground-level nest. I peeked into Gabriela's room, admired her Nobel medal, and then headed to the wide, round fountain with water spilling in the center. I sat on a bench, where a small, mud-colored cat joined me. I stroked his head and wondered how he was allowed to wander freely in this garden, populated by doves, chickens, and peacocks. When he jumped up onto the edge of the fountain, I thought, *Uh-oh. The fish!* But all he wanted was to drink some water. That assortment of animals living in harmony seemed so appropriate for that church and monastery named in honor of St. Francis.

I had a view across the garden to the opposite corridor and the second floor, the monastery corridors forming a square enclosing the garden. Above the roof, in the distance, rose a glass skyscraper tapering into a needle tip. The roar of buses' revving engines passing on the Alameda carried over the thick walls. I tried to imagine what life had been like for the monks who first planted these trees, which now, centuries later, provided me with a shady oasis of serenity. Undoubtedly, clad in their thick rough brown robes, they lived spartan lives within those adobe walls. No heat in their bare cells, simple fare on their communal tables crafted by their own hands. I imagine they had a division of labor: some more skilled in baking bread, others in carpentry, and a few who were drawn to the inner courtyard to set out edible plants, fruit trees, and this leafy cork tree under which I sit today.

X. SINGING LOVE

Only he who loves can sing. *Love can spark the desire to sing joyfully—first love, unexpected love, familial love— while a ballad of heartbreak tells of lost love. Whatever the circumstances—whether we're the one giving love or receiving or, better yet, both—the experience alters us and its memories live on, becoming a part of who we are.*

The Fox and His Rose

His smooth, olive hands bore no ring. His appearance gave no clue about his age or job. He was sitting by the window, and I took the seat next to him. Exchanging smiles and *buenas tardes*, we settled back for the long flight over the jungles and mountains of Central America.

We introduced ourselves. I told him I'd been back visiting the barrio in Colombia, where I'd served two years earlier as a Peace Corps volunteer, and was now headed to Mexico to travel with a friend. He was Alfonso, he said, from Ecuador.

"But I'm called Tata Poncho by the Indian villagers where I work, in Mexico."

"What do you do there?"

"I'm an anthropologist . . . and a Jesuit priest."

At age twenty-five, I was meeting my first anthropologist, a profession I linked in my mind with exotic cultures. Here was a cultured man whom I wanted to get to know. It felt like it was mutual—but he was a priest.

Oblivious to the passing landscape below, we became absorbed in conversation like two people on our own planet. Sometime later, he pointed out the stars in the darkness outside. He motioned for me to lean across him to get a glimpse. I wondered if he sensed our physical closeness, as I did in those stargazing moments.

"How beautiful." I leaned back into my seat, settling a little nearer to him.

He smiled. "They remind me of the story *The Little Prince*."

I admitted that I hadn't read it.

"It's a wonderful tale," Alfonso said. He told me of the Little

Prince's visits to the different planets, lingering over his encounter with the fox, who explains how the Little Prince can tame him little by little by moving closer to the fox each day. The fox then reminds the Little Prince that, once he has domesticated something, like his rose at home, he will always be responsible for it. When it is time to part, the Little Prince, noting the fox's sadness, asks what good it has done him to be tamed. The fox replies that whenever he looks at the wheat fields, he'll remember the color of the Little Prince's hair.

The pilot's voice interrupted our conversation, announcing our arrival in Mexico City. I remembered the friend waiting for me at the airport and wished him away. In the terminal, Alfonso and I embraced, wishing each other well. He gave me his card with an address.

Music was everywhere in Mexico, on buses, in shops, and on the streets. Spanish singer Raphael's soulful voice haunted me, singing *"Hablemos de Amor."* I convinced my traveling companion to visit the village where Tata Poncho worked, hoping to see him again, but the news was disappointing. He had not yet returned from Mexico City.

Unpacking back in California, I came across Alfonso's card and wrote him a note: "So sorry to have missed you." I bought an album of Raphael's love songs. One day, a thin brown package with Mexican postage arrived. I pulled off the paper to find a Spanish copy of *The Little Prince.* Inside, Alfonso wrote, "To Susanita from your fox, who will always be responsible for his rose." "Always" was underlined. "I hope we'll meet again someday. Alfonso. 1970."

Sometimes I take the book from the shelf, its paper cover now tattered and faded, read his words, and recall the man who'll always be my fox.

Dream Lover

Walking back from Pilates class with a friend this morning, I brought up the topic of sex and senior citizens. I'd had a vivid, erotic dream the previous night. After a long lapse of time, I dreamed once again of Peter, my first heartthrob. We were holding and kissing each other, but I held back. I wanted to make certain of the honesty of his intentions. He'd burned me once, more than fifty years earlier.

I laughed, "He's probably fat and bald now!"

My friend said, "Google him."

I met Peter, a senior, my first week as a student at Berkeley. I was seventeen, fresh out of Catholic high school. Despite my minimal dating experience, the most handsome hunk in the men's dorm was asking me out! I could see the window of his room from mine, and he'd lean out the window and whistle for me. I remember our first kiss, during a nighttime walk under the campus campanile. We'd park in the Berkeley hills and make out with the glistening lights of the San Francisco Bay Area spread out below us.

But all wasn't roses. I learned from the girls in my dorm that he had a long-term girlfriend, living in another dorm. He was burning the candle at both ends. The canceled dates now had an explanation. Toward the end of that year, he broke off our relationship. He'd made his choice.

For the following two years, my love life was dreary. Although I had an occasional date, I couldn't get Peter out of my system. I received sporadic, noncommittal letters from him, telling me of his days training as a navy pilot, signed just "Pete." I didn't understand why he was writing to me. There was no way I could read into his words that he still had feelings for me. I didn't answer. It was too painful, yet I've kept his letters all these years.

My senior year, I finally recovered from the heartbreak and was able to move on when I began dating Juan Carlos, an enchanting Cuban student. There were other men in my life while I worked as a Peace Corps volunteer in the steamy climate of coastal Colombia.

Returning to California, I lived the life of a carefree Berkeley spirit, independent and single. Then I met a handsome Chilean and moved to his country to marry him. Sometimes I'd dream about an encounter with Peter, the one who got away. What would it be like to see him again? But those fantasies faded with time.

My friend's suggestion to Google him nagged at me during the day. That dream was so vivid, so real. I thought, *Why not?* I sat down at the computer and typed his name and city. A photo and vital information immediately appeared on the screen. It was his obituary. He'd passed away just months earlier. He'd worked as a navy pilot, married the girlfriend from college, and had two children and four grandchildren. Just like me. I was glad for him. A photo showed a tanned, handsome man. Donations were requested for an Alzheimer's fund.

Though he'd been absent from my life for decades, he had remained present deep in my memory. I suppose I'd assumed that he was still living his life somewhere and that maybe, once in a while, he thought of me. Now I felt as if I'd had the wind knocked out of me. Suddenly, age and mortality became very real.

So why now, did I, a woman in her seventies, have such a vivid dream about Peter—a dream with strong feelings and longing that continued into wakefulness?

I believe he came to say goodbye. I might have expected a tender, affectionate farewell for old times' sake, but not those passionate, tender embraces that I'd struggled for years to forget.

La Llorona

Entertaining my three granddaughters when they come to our house doesn't require much imagination or effort. What we mainly do is play. Among their favorite pastimes are drawing, playing house, and racing the Matchbox cars that belonged to their dad. We've also invented a few games that they never tire of.

There's Monsters and Animals, which involves pushing, shoving, and tickling on top of their grandparents' bed.

"I'm an alligator with sharp teeth."

"I'm a hippo with a huge mouth."

"And I'm a lion with long claws."

And we roll and tickle and shove and laugh until Grandmother calls time out for a rest.

Another all-time favorite is our version of "Jack and the Beanstalk." They call the game Fee-Fi-Fo-Fum. I, the giant, stomp around the house, hunting for them in their hiding places, while I growl, "Fee-fi-fo-fum." Their giggling usually gives them away, followed by screams when I find them and threaten to take a bite out of a plump arm or leg.

Last week, we played a Latin American version. We had just watched a Mexican movie, *La Llorona,* based on a legend of Maria. Her children had drowned, and she was destined to haunt the villages at night in a shroud, wailing for them and kidnapping village children. I learned of the legend years ago in California and heard the song "*La Llorona*" on Mexican radio stations. But Santiago had never heard of it.

Throwing a large dark blue shawl over my head, I announced to the girls, "*Soy la llorona.* I'm the *llorona.*" With hysterical screams, they ran off to find hiding places. I wailed throughout the house, discovering their curled-up bodies in dark closet corners, behind armchairs, and finally under their grandfather's office desk, as he tried to put on an innocent face.

My granddaughters grant me a priceless gift—occasions for the child in me to come out and play. I hope, when the girls are grown, they'll remember playing *La Llorona* with their grandmother.

XI. THE REALM
OF MAGIC REALISM

Only while reading Cien Años de Soledad *in Spanish have I been able to look back on my time in Colombia and comprehend why it is the home of magic realism, a world that blends the supernatural with that of the natural and familiar. In the book and in my memories, there is no clear line separating the real from the magical. There was something mysterious and mythical in the hordes of flying cockroaches; the house-shaking, deafening claps of thunder; the cackle of the old woman next door. The perspective of the years has allowed me to perceive the marvelous and the fantastical in that tropical landscape, pulsating with the deafening buzz of cicadas ensconced under leaves like green umbrellas, and the trombone calls of the nighttime frogs, endowing that mulatto world with mystical traits, phantasmagorical images undulating on waves of heat.*

Journey to the Unknown

It's 2015, and I've done it: reserved a flight for Barranquilla, Colombia, in three weeks' time. For years, I've longed to return to my barrio in Barranquilla. Even after five decades, the imprint those experiences left remains strong: the warmth of the people, the suffocating heat and pervasive humidity, the fragrance of ripe mangoes, the lilt of the coastal accent, the music, and the wonderful, wild cacophony of the frogs in the night.

A formal invitation in Spanish had arrived by email, announcing a ceremony, to be held in Barranquilla, commemorating a total of twenty-five years of Peace Corps service in Colombia. Not twenty-five consecutive years, though, as it was long considered unsafe to send volunteers there because of *la violencia*, years of leftist guerilla warfare.

I've been filled with apprehension while making this decision. Browsing the Internet, I learn about the new reality of the city and the barrio of Las Américas. It's difficult to take in. The last time I was there, Internet didn't exist. Now I can roam the barrio's streets via Google Earth. Some roads are now paved, and shacks have become solidly built, though still humble, homes. Las Américas began as a squatter barrio, a shantytown with no plan or organization. I once knew my way in the dark through the labyrinth of dirt roads. Now I would lose my way.

My doubts peak with an email from the Barranquilla Peace Corps office responding to my inquiries. Las Américas is now considered a "red zone," off-limits to Peace Corps volunteers, for safety reasons. I read online news items of criminals, murders, and gang fights. But there is also news of large new schools, a football program for kids, and a new health center (the first one was my last project while working there). Besides, I'm a *for-mer* volunteer; their rules no longer apply to me.

I will persist. I'm open to adventure. Flaco (Skinny) Bob, from my old training group, emails that he is going, too, and offers to accompany me on my searches. He knows the city well and has contacts. I dig out old letters and photos and jot down names and the address of my godson, from whom I last heard in 1996. Will I be able to locate my dear friends Petra and Fidelia in Las Américas? I have no addresses for them. No one used street names or house numbers in those years.

Onboard Avianca flight 98, I'm now headed to Bogotá and then Barranquilla. The map on the screen on the seat back in front of me indicates we are over the desert of northern Chile—in spectacular bloom after an unusual rainy winter.

I haven't been back there since my early twenties and now experience the feeling—with certain trepidations—that I'm returning to my past. Diaphanous clouds of memories drift through my head, of my last visit to see Dominga and my barrio friends.

It's 1969. The red-white-and-blue-striped, blimp-shaped vehicle grinds and roars, lurching and rolling from side to side with the jerking movements of an armored tank. Periodically, it lunges to a stop to suck in a group of people through an opening at the front. Out of the back of the bus, a clutch of riders tumbles, as if from a giant exhaust pipe.

It's the barrio bus taking me back. I've returned from California for a visit one year after completing my two-year assignment as a Peace Corps volunteer in Barrio Las Américas. Gripping the seat back in front of me, I recall the first time I made the trip as a newly sworn-in volunteer. I was amazed by the utter sameness of everything: block after block, mile after mile, of drab, mud-splattered, slouching houses, lining each side of the rut-filled road. Without any distinct landmarks to guide me, I knew I'd be lost in the maze. It was a month before I dared go out alone.

I finally learned to use the neighborhood stores as the handiest, most frequent landmarks. Now that I'm in Barranquilla again, I look for the familiar Spanish names: *Así es la Vida* (That's Life); *la Esquina Caliente* (the Hot Corner); *la Lucha* (the Struggle). I remember that one. And there's *la Fuente de Oro* (the Fountain of Gold). This is where I get off.

"*Próxima!*" I call to the driver.

I hurry along the two blocks of dirt road to Dominga's one-room brick house. Dear Dominga, my cigar-smoking mulatta, erstwhile housemate, and surrogate mother. There she is in the doorway, watching for me.

The past year, I've struggled with a perplexing culture shock. I've felt like a social misfit. Juan, the Berkeley boyfriend with whom I corresponded throughout my two years in Barranquilla, suddenly stopped calling me. I earned my teaching credential but now am unsure I even want to teach. Neither jobs nor boyfriends are on my horizon. All that insecurity now fades as Dominga wraps her brown arms around me. Inside, she pulls back the curtain separating her bed from the all-purpose sitting-eating area, where, over two kerosene burners, *sancocho* soup simmers. I am to sleep in her bed, she tells me; she'll string up her hammock. She waves a broom to chase out a brown hen that has wandered in from the backyard. *Fuera!* Out! The next morning, we have a great laugh when I discover the same hen roosting inside my open suitcase.

The following day, I'm eager to visit Las Américas and start down the steep, eroded dirt road leading into the barrio, wondering how I will find things. Outwardly, the most noticeable change is the arrival of electricity, including streetlights. But the roads that I walked so often in the searing sun and the precarious shacks are unchanged.

I spend the afternoon visiting my closest friends. One is Petra, a cheerful, golden-skinned woman who wears her wavy black hair in two long braids down her back. She is surprised to see me.

"Señorita Susana! When did you arrive?"

"Today."

"You came back fat!"

Plumpness is a sign of good health. Colombians are anxious that you eat well to show that you are content in their country. When I'm invited to one of my barrio friend's home, the lady of the house serves enormous helpings and stands by, watching to make sure that I eat every last bit of the mountains of rice, yucca, fried plantains, and potatoes. Only then is she satisfied.

"How have you been, Petra?"

"Fair."

"What's new?"

"*Nada.*"

"You mean nothing has happened in a whole year?"

"Well, we have a new baby. Come and meet Rosita."

This conversation is repeated, almost word for word, at every house I visit. I learn of births (some young members of the women's committee are married and have their first babies) and of early deaths (those of Jesus Quiroz, a hard worker at community projects, and Oswaldo Hernández, a small man with sparkling blue eyes and a bushy mustache).

I stop by the house of Juan Bermudez, the president of the community-action junta. He isn't home, but the mother of his six children, Eugenia, invites me in. The three-room, unpainted clapboard shack is furnished with a few chairs, a table, a bed, cots, and a hammock. Several swollen-bellied children sit bare-bottomed on the dirt floor, mouths dirt-smudged, noses dripping, hair thin and stringy. Eugenia's skin is pale and blemished, her hair unwashed and uncombed, her body slouched inside a shapeless black skirt and faded blouse safety-pinned across her bony chest. Her eyes are red-rimmed and watery from the smoke of the cook fire on the floor in the rear of the house.

During my visit, she opens herself to me. The subject of birth control comes up. "I don't want any more children. This is enough. Things are becoming too much for me. Look at me. I'm only twenty-eight years old, but I look like an old woman."

A few years older than I am, she looks closer to forty. Contrary to superficial impressions, within her frail, worn body breathes the spirit of a young woman. Her greatest tragedy is her awareness of the frightening reality of what she has become. Later I ask Juan why he doesn't move the fire outside or build a small stove with a chimney. He is planning to one of these days, he says.

Dominga's daughter, Herminda, asks me to be the godmother of her newborn son, Jose. Now, as their *comadre*, I am part of the family. When it's time for the teary goodbyes, I hate seeing Dominga so sad and promise her I'll return soon. We'll keep in touch by letters, as before. Because she is illiterate, she dictates her letters to her oldest grandson and he will read mine to her.

Every month or so, a pale blue air-mail envelope bearing the Barranquilla postmark arrives with one folded sheet inside.

This paper trail is all that connects Dominga and me now, the letter in my hand a tangible expression of our deep, ongoing friendship.

It will all be changed now. Will they have running water? Indoor toilets? Will I be able to locate my old friends or Dominga's daughter or my godson, Jose?

And I am now a white-haired grandmother. Will they recognize me? This is a journey to many unknowns. The people and places that populate my nostalgia no longer exist as I remember them. Will I be disappointed? Dear Dominga passed away years ago. My shadowy memories must confront reality and make peace with it, but I'm reluctant to give up the scenes in my memory. Of course, I hope not to find the dire poverty of those years. The airplane magazine reveals a modern Colombia of malls and pricey condos. Yet I fear that something will have been lost in the name of progress. But the past and the present must meet—it's a gap I must bridge.

I am not the same person now, not just physically. Young, idealistic, and ruled by raging hormones in that sultry, suffocating, relentless climate, I went there to give of myself, to help the less fortunate, but I was the one who came away the richer. Now, knowing that my time there will be short, my only expectations are to revisit that place and renew those friendships that marked me forever.

We land in gray, cloudy Bogotá. Tears well up. I wend my way through the airport and board my connection to Barranquilla. The flight will be just over an hour. The landscape I view from my window tells me we're getting close. There's the wide, meandering Magdalena River and the broad expanses of flat, marshy countryside.

I emerge from the Barranquilla airport into a mass of hot air, the searing, humid climate I remember so vividly. I look around for Bob, who said he'd try to meet me here. Soon I'm the only passenger left so I board a small yellow taxi, which careens, honking, through heavy traffic on unfamiliar streets. "What barrio is this?" I ask the driver, but the name means nothing. I feel like a complete stranger visiting the city for the first time, a city I once knew so well. Only the iconic El Prado Hotel, sixty-five years old, as elegant as I recall and the place I'd go for R and R, is familiar. In the lobby, some gringos look at me and ask, "Peace Corps?" With relief, I learn they are staff, and they offer to take me to the Peace Corps office to meet others who have gathered for the commemoration event.

At last, connected.

Red Zone

"Jorge Romero is the one to talk to," they say.

I'm on the sixth floor of the bustling city hall of Barranquilla and eager to begin my search. I have only a week.

"Where is Jorge Romero?" I ask at the front desk, and am directed to a man at a desk nearby.

I introduce myself. "Señor Romero, I sent you an email several weeks ago."

He lifts his gaze from his computer, "Yes, I received your email."

"You didn't answer me."

"Elections are this Sunday, and it's been a very busy time."

"Can you help me? I'd like to contact the president of the junta in Barrio Las Américas. I want to go there and need someone from the barrio to accompany me. People tell me it's dangerous."

He checks his computer and writes down the president's name, address, and cell phone number. (Telephones in Las Américas!) Then he picks up his phone. He's calling Alfonso, the president, explaining who I am and that I will be contacting him.

"How do I get there?" I ask. "I checked out the barrio on Google Earth. It's so changed now. I'd get lost."

He prints out a Google map and traces a line on it for the taxi to follow.

Jorge Romero, I could kiss you.

That evening, I call Alfonso. "Jorge Romero told me to contact you. I lived and worked in Las Américas as a Peace Corps volunteer many years ago."

"*Sí*, I've heard of you. You helped build the health center."
He knows who I am!

"Would it be possible for me to visit there? I need someone to show me around, as I'm certain it's quite changed."

"I'm running for office in Sunday's elections, so I'm pretty busy, but I'd be happy to meet with you the day after tomorrow."

We make plans to get together at his house. Since I promised Santiago I wouldn't go there alone, I ask Flaco Bob to accompany me.

Bob and I flag down one of the ubiquitous yellow Chevrolet Spark taxis that swarm through the city like indomitable bees. I ask the driver if he's willing to go to Barrio Las Américas. "I have this map," I say, handing it to him. Despite the Peace Corps warnings that it's a "red zone," I'm skeptical. Maybe I just don't want to believe it.

The driver checks the map several times and then turns left off the wide, busy street we've been following for twenty minutes. Not the route I used to take on the bus. "This is Las Américas," he says.

I stare out the window in shock and disappointment. Solidly built, modest houses line both sides of a paved street. Nothing is familiar. No remembered landmarks: the corner stores, the slope leading to the church, the road the buses traveled, the leaning wooden houses. Where is the barrio of my memories?

We pull up to Alfonso's house, its facade papered with a huge ad promoting him for city *edil* in Sunday's elections. (I have to look that one up. *Aedile*: a magistrate in ancient Rome, in charge of public works, buildings, and roads.) A young man appears in the open doorway, wearing a T-shirt proclaiming *Junta de Acción Comunal Las Américas*. We shake hands, and he invites Bob and me inside. The bare cement walls and floor look freshly constructed.

"Las Américas is so changed," I tell Alfonso. I pull an envelope out of my purse. "I noticed on the city's web page that you wrote a short history of the barrio. I've brought copies of some old photos for you, so you can see what the barrio was like then." I hand him a faded, black-and-white picture. "Here are the men working on the health center, and this one shows the inauguration."

He studies the photos. "You know, we have a new health center now. I'll take you there."

"And the original health center we built?"

"We'll go by there as well," he says.

I'm anxious to see it. At least *it* will look familiar. Such sacrifice and sweat went into its construction. My parents held a fund-raiser to pay for the roof.

We step outside, into the shade of a tree. I look around. Instead of wooden shacks perched precariously on rolling hills of eroded, barren red soil, I see trees, vegetation, and cinder-block houses. A few shacks remain like the one next door to Alfonso, where, he tells me, three families live. I tell Bob, "That's what all the houses were like when I worked here."

Several women wander up, including Alfonso's sister and his mother, a small, sweet-faced woman wearing a white T-shirt with the image of a saint and the saint's name, Santa María Goretti. She doesn't hesitate to pose for photos. Alfonso introduces me to the gathering, explaining that I'm the one who helped build the old health center. More join us, as if notified through a barrio grapevine. They stare at me with mild curiosity. I immediately forget their names. Not one is familiar. Alfonso passes the photos around.

The little group livens. "Look, there's my father!" says one neighbor. They crowd around to look at the picture. "The one there, with the mustache." I recognize her face but not her name.

"This way, Señora Susana," says Alfonso, and we start off down a paved street like visiting dignitaries, escorted by our emissaries, Alfonso and his sister.

On a corner under a tree, some young men in blue jeans and T-shirts hang out with their motorcycles. Uh-oh. The term "red zone" pops up in my mind like a warning flag. But Alfonso walks up to them and introduces me. "These men drive moto-taxis," he explains. He shows them the photos I've brought. They pass them around, pointing out cousins, fathers, old neighbors.

"That's what Las Américas looked like fifty years ago," I tell them.

Amid laughter, we crowd together for photos, in which I perch on a motorcycle seat. I even consider the possibility of arranging a ride back to the hotel later with one of them, until I recall the recklessness of the motorcyclists downtown.

Alfonso moves our little party along. "Let's go down this street where Señora Nidia lives." Nidia, a familiar name.

Older women, in faded shorts and skirts, T-shirts, and flip-flops, drift out of neighboring houses. Again names flit by, airborne words I cannot grasp. Most remember me, and I regret that I don't remember them. I want to. But I worked mainly with men when I was here, all of whom, I learn, are now dead.

"Oh, yes, my mother used to talk about Señorita Susana."

"My grandmother spoke of you."

"You knew my mother. I'm the daughter of Modesta Borerro."

"Of course! Señora Modesta," I say. "She always dressed in black and had a sickly grandchild, Doris."

"Doris is married now and has children."

I find this news hard to imagine. Doris was a severely malnourished infant, blind in one eye. We gather in a semicircle for multiple photos, our arms linked. A woman crosses the street toward us. "Here's Nancy Vasquez," someone says.

"Señora Susana!"

"Nancy!" We hug and laugh. She was a teenager in a women's group we organized back then. Now she is a thin woman with a weathered face, but I still recognize in her countenance the young girl in the photo I show her. Alfonso urges us on. I know his time is limited, but I want to stay and chat with these women, discover people we knew in common and ask more about their lives, desires, and hopes. This fast-paced barrio tour is not allowing me to get below the surface, to *connect* and feel as if I belong here once more.

"I'd like to see the old health center," I tell him. "My friends Fidelia and Petra lived on the same street." Because none of the houses is familiar, we ask at various doorways for Fidelia and Petra, but the news is not good. Both have passed away.

"There's the old health center," says Alfonso. But I can't really *see* it. The one place I thought would be familiar is boarded up, the construction now considered unsafe. Although I'm terribly disappointed, I take comfort in knowing that it served the community for several decades and now, though it will take on a new form, is destined to continue as an homage to the men and women who struggled and sacrificed to make their health center a reality.

But when Alfonso takes us to see the new facility, the large, modern structure looks out of place, as if some city official plunked it down by mistake. How is it possible? *This* in Las Américas?

In the spacious, immaculate, air-conditioned interior, Alfonso introduces me to the doctor and a nurse. I'm thrilled when the doctor tells me that he used to work in the old health center; in doing so, he reveals his dedication to this community, something that many doctors might avoid.

Several patients are waiting their turn. One older woman smiles and waves. "I remember you! I'm the wife of the owner of the Turbaco store."

"Of course," I say. "We held meetings and dances there." But later, when Alfonso points out the corner store, it looks nothing like the one I remember.

We visit a "megaschool," one of two that receive children from prekindergarten age through high school. Neatly uniformed boys and girls chatter and scurry through the hallways. A tussle erupts between two young boys. "He hit me with his backpack." Hallway bulletin boards carry messages about democratic values and beneficial environmental practices. Our tour includes the gym and cafeteria, where the students are served lunch. Alfonso introduces me to the school director, a small, middle-aged man with a very long gray beard. He explains that a Canadian Baptist organization founded and runs the school.

"Are all these children from Las Américas?" I ask, disbelieving.

He assures me they are. I'm delighted. Again we pose for photos. We peek into a room, where the littlest ones are napping on mats. As we leave, I congratulate the director on the magnificent work they do.

Bob comments that my face is very red. Beads of perspiration slide down my neck, my arms, under my bra, but I can't say no when Alfonso says I must see the church, which I do remember, and meet the priest. Adjacent to the Catholic church is the Escuela Golda Meir, founded by the Barranquilla Jewish women's community.

I'm elated to see the many improvements in infrastructure and services in the barrio: running water, schools, health centers, football fields, and some paved streets. But, talking to the neighbors, I realize that most of these improvements have occurred only in the past decade, under the administrations of the past two, civic-minded mayors. But the houses? No politician could claim credit for them. It was each determined, hardworking family that labored to convert its flimsy shack into a solid house, cement block by cement block.

Alfonso is busy with elections just four days off, so I suggest we find a taxi. "But I don't want to leave until I've seen Agripina," I tell Bob. "She was another thirteen-year-old in our women's group." Alfonso directs the driver up a rocky incline to a small, run-down house. He announces my arrival to Agripina. I pass through the front door of peeling brown paint into a drab living room, equipped with a few basic pieces of furniture. I never would have recognized her without the introduction. How can this gaunt, bent, and flat-chested woman be the same person as the perky, smiling girl with hopeful eyes in the photo I carry? We embrace.

"How have you been, Agripina?"

"Not so well. It's my back. Gives me a lot of pain."

"Have you been to the health center?"

"Yes, but I can't pay for the medicine."

I know then that I'll send her some money.

We pose for the camera against the backdrop of a cracked, patched wall and a lopsided painting. I show her the black-and-white snapshot I brought. It is my only copy, but it is all I have to give to her. "Do you remember this day in my house? We were making hand puppets."

She nods. I tell her that I regret that my visit is so brief, but the taxi waits outside. We hug farewell.

I feel as if a whirlwind has whisked me through the barrio, a dream run in fast forward. So many more questions. I hoped someone might invite me back another day, for a more leisurely visit. I wanted to visit Eugenia, the former president's wife, now a widow. I remember her house and the deplorable conditions in which I saw her decades ago, yet she outlived her husband.

We drop off Alfonso and his sister at a corner. I thank him and wish him *suerte* in the upcoming elections. Although I'm on the verge of sun stroke, I lament that this will be my only visit to this place that marked me with such an outpouring of love—then and now.

Mangrove Marshes, Mosquitoes, and a Motorcycle

The next-to-last day of my Barranquilla sojourn. I've arranged to meet early this morning with Omar, a guide at Isla de Salamanca National Park, to go bird watching.

"*Cómo llego?* How do I get there?" I ask him on the phone.

"Take the bus from the terminal to Santa Marta, but ask the driver to let you off at Los Cocos, or the park, just four kilometers past the tollbooth."

Milling passengers swarm through the bus terminal. I find a ticket office for buses to Santa Marta. Bus 3039 is about to leave. A friendly young man helps me locate it in the line of buses outside.

I sit in a seat right behind the driver to make sure he understands where I want to get off. As if I know.

Forty minutes later, the bus slows and the driver's assistant nods to me. I step out onto the edge of the two-lane highway, shimmering with heat waves and bordered with a mass of green vegetation, palm trees poking up their spiky, disheveled fronds in the distance. I look about, seeing nothing but a PARK sign.

"Susana!" a voice calls, and off a side road steps a dark-haired young man, skin the shade of *café con leche*, a camera hung around his neck. I presume this is Omar. We shake hands, and I follow him into the park. Ahead, on the terrace of a small building, a group of young people sit around tables.

"English classes," Omar says. "They are tourism students." He introduces me to the teacher, who announces to the class that they have before them a native English speaker. They twitter and stare.

"Would you please talk to them about the importance of learning English?" asks the teacher.

I've come to bird-watch and now must say something inspiring to these eager students. I manage to say how English facilitates travel in almost every country, as well as increases employment opportunities. The teacher seems satisfied. They all clap.

Omar hands me binoculars, and I follow him into the park. He has an acute ear for bird calls and excitedly points out among the branches our first feathered sighting. He announces that it's a *Parkesia noveboracensis*.

"Omar, *por favor*, what's the common name for it?"

I expect him to provide me with the local name. Instead, he opens his English-language field guide to Colombian birds, points to the image of the northern water thrush, and attempts to pronounce it in English. I correct his pronunciation, but his tongue stumbles over the *thr* in "thrush."

"You must put your tongue between your teeth, like this," I demonstrate, exaggerating the sound. *"Tthhrrrr."* He tells me he's very anxious to learn and continues struggling to pronounce the birds' names in English.

The park is unexpectedly dry below the tree canopy. It hasn't rained much, Omar tells me. He points out the three different types of mangrove trees in the park. I snap photos of their grabbing, snakelike roots. It becomes clear that this is also mosquito land. In spite of having lavished abundant insect repellent on all exposed skin, we both swat our way through the groves and past the *ciénegas*, wide marshes ringed by thick vegetation. He points to a path formed at night by the *caimánes*, the crocodiles. The deeper into the park we go, and the more my eyes grow accustomed to the light and the colors, the more birds we spot.

The sighting of an unbelievably camouflaged nighthawk is a high point.

When we finish the circuit of trails, I ask Omar to help me make a list of what we have seen, seventeen species in all, including sandpipers, parakeets, wood creepers, flycatchers, woodpeckers, and the spectacular russet-throated puff bird.

I thank Omar, pay him, and ask, "How do I get back to Barranquilla now?"

"We sit by the highway and flag down the bus."

We sit on the curb in a spot of shade and wait. Trucks, cars, and fancy buses speed by, but not the local bus that would stop here, in the middle of nowhere, to take on a passenger. The blazing midday sun is well overhead when Omar says maybe I'll have to catch the bus at the town of Palomar.

"And how do I get there?" I ask, tired and sweaty, trying not to scratch the growing red welts on my legs.

"I'll flag down my friend who has a moto-taxi. He's very trustworthy."

At this point, I'd accept a ride on a burro.

Soon his friend putts up. Omar explains the situation, and the driver agrees. He hands me a grimy helmet and holds out his hand to help me onto the back of his motorcycle.

"Where do I put my hands?"

"Around my waist," the young man answers, and off we putt.

The rush of air is soothing, and I try to relax and enjoy the view. *Oh, if my husband could see me now.* Omar's friend is careful with his white-haired, pale-faced passenger, sticking to the edge of the road. I wonder how fast we're going and look down at the speedometer. Zero kilometers per hour? The gas gauge needle points at *E*. Empty. What if we run out of gas? Then it dawns on me that this moto-taxi is a patchwork hybrid, likely put together "one piece at a time," like Johnny Cash's Cadillac. After fifteen or twenty minutes, I wonder how far this town of Palomar is. Maybe Omar's friend isn't as trustworthy as he claimed. Is he planning to take me hostage? When we pass the tollbooth, I know we're nearing the wide Magdalena River. This is much farther than I thought. What a relief when my driver slows and stops by a clutch of roadside stands. In less than a minute, a bus sporting tropical colors emerges from a side road.

"There it is. Once in town, you must get off at *calle* seventeen and take a taxi from there," he announces, and waves to the driver to stop.

I climb aboard. A woman with a child gestures me to sit next to her in the front row. I'm tickled. This is the kind of bus I used to ride here fifty years ago. A green fringe edges the windshield, and stuffed toy animals—a bear, a dog, a rabbit, an elephant— dangle and sway from the roof over the driver's area. His seat is upholstered in a blue plastic, fringed material. We sway in our seats to the rhythm of coastal music—*vallenatos, cumbias*— blaring from loudspeakers behind the driver. Warm air blows through the open door.

This is what I've come for.

Searching for Jose

Dominga's grandson, the godson I knew only as an infant, wrote me periodically for many years, but now all I have is an address on a letter written nineteen years ago.

I give the taxi driver the address in Barrio El Carmen, explaining my story. "I don't know if my godson still lives there." We locate the street and the house number. Several workers mill about in front of the house, which is being remodeled and is clearly unoccupied.

The driver says, "Ask the neighbors."

"Do you know what happened to the Castillo Rocha family who used to live here?"

Heads shake. "No, no one by that name. Ask that woman across the street. She's been here a long time."

"No, sorry."

Back in the taxi, I tell the driver, "I have his parents' address. Can you take me there? It's in Barrio La Sierra."

This is my last hope.

Street numbers are confusing: 45A, 45B, 45C. "Where's 45D?" we ask a passerby. We drive in circles along streets of broken asphalt. A cab driver explains the street numbers were changed; 45D is now 50.

Another slow circle around the block, and then . . . "There it is!"

The driver stops. I pay him but ask him to wait to make sure I've got the right house, a solidly built house, not the hut of tin planks I remember.

At the padlocked gate, I wave to a figure inside the open front door.

"*Haló?* Is this the house of the Castillo Rocha family?"

She nods yes.

"I'm Jose's *madrina.*"

A young woman I don't recognize comes to open the gate. I give a thumbs-up to the driver.

Inside, I'm shocked to come face-to-face with an exact but older version of Dominga. It's Herminda, her daughter, now in her eighties. We hug and laugh. The other woman is Consuelo, her daughter-in-law, wife of their son Jorge. They live here, too, along with their disabled daughter, Adriana. Soon Herminda's husband, Miguel, appears. More hugs. I tell them of my search to find Jose's house.

"Oh, he moved years ago. Let's call him on the phone."

Miguel dials and talks to Jose, explaining that his *madrina* is here. Unexpected. Unannounced. He hands me the phone. What shall I say?

"*Hola,* Jose. *Sorpresa!*"

"*Madrina!* Yes, this is a surprise! When did you arrive?"

I explain how I hunted for his house. We decide that I will go in a taxi with his parents in two days' time to his house and meet his family. He has to work tomorrow, and I have the Peace Corps commemorative event.

Consuelo brings me a cool lemonade, and we sit and talk in the breeze of an electric fan. I ask to use the bathroom. They show me to a real indoor version.

"Come to meet Adriana." Consuelo leads me into a bedroom, where Adriana's distorted body is propped on pillows on a bed, an electric fan directed toward her. Her eyes open occasionally. She makes soft grunting sounds. She was born perfectly healthy, Consuelo tells me, but contracted encephalitis at a year's age. That was eighteen years ago.

"*Hola*, Adriana," I say, and caress her arm.

"Would you like me to take a picture of her?" I ask.

Her mother nods. I search for the words to tell her how difficult it must be for her to care for Adriana and am pleased to hear that they have a visiting doctor and therapist. I also notice a folded wheelchair propped in the back patio.

We finalize plans for our visit with Jose. They call me a cab. Miguel warns me to set the price with the driver before leaving.

At the Peace Corps anniversary event the following day, posters with photos of the projects of past and present volunteers are displayed on the walls of the meeting hall. We veteran volunteers are identifiable by our gray heads. Bob and Margery are the only ones from my old group, but we introduce ourselves to the others and ask the inevitable questions: What years were you here? Where were you posted? I realize that we really were pioneers, among the first Peace Corps volunteers to arrive in Colombia. Now, from my perspective, the current young volunteers seem more protected. Learning that they must live with a Colombian family, that they mainly teach English and that they are no longer assigned to urban areas because of safety concerns, I appreciate how much freer of restrictions we were then.

Speeches by local and Peace Corps dignitaries and the large presence of Colombian guests make clear that this event has been designed to familiarize the audience with the history of the Peace Corps there and its aim to grow in numbers after the long absence. The new PC director, the first woman, awards a pin to each of us old-timers. This day, I come to the realization that I was part of something important and historic.

The next day, I hire a taxi and stop to pick up Herminda and Miguel, who, I now realize, are both hard of hearing. Miguel directs the driver until we pull up in front of a small, attached, one-story house facing an unfenced dirt soccer field.

With only old letters and a twenty-year-old photo, I have no expectations of what my godson will look like or what kind of person he has become. When a tall, very thin man with dark eyes comes toward me, I can't hide my surprise. He bears little resemblance to Herminda or Miguel or to his mulatta grand-mother, Dominga—yet there is something familiar about him.

"You're Jose?"

He smiles and nods.

"You're so thin! I would never have guessed that you're Dominga's grandson!"

He laughs. "Everyone tells me I should eat more."

We hug each other tightly. Although we are virtual strangers, I sense an immediate and deep connection, as if we've known each other all our lives. Perhaps in a way we have, through our mutual affection for Dominga. I suspect she is practicing a touch of sorcery from the beyond. In this land of magic realism, anything is possible. Now Jose is a forty-eight-year-old man with four children and a granddaughter.

He addresses me as Madrina and introduces me to his wife, Evelyn; her mother; his seven-year-old, Miguel Ángel; his daughter, Kiara, who's leaving for her nursing job; and Angie, a married daughter, whose toddler naps in a bedroom. Kevin, the sixteen-year-old, is out studying but arrives later, a handsome young man.

We sit in a tiny front patio under two mango trees and talk of our lives and our families. From her cage hung in a tree, their parrot, Lucía, tilts her head, as if following the conversation, and occasionally contributes an opinion. Several potted plants line the tiled patio, dividing it from their neighbors'. "The plants are Jose's," says Evelyn.

"I water them before work," he says, "and spray Lucía and her cage with the hose while I'm at it." Later, we go to a narrow strip of back patio to see their parakeets and a finch.

"Jose," I tell him, "we have the same interests."

His wife remarks that they have a family joke that Jose, because of his narrow face and nose, is really my son, and that I left him with Herminda to care for.

I don't feel motherly toward him. It's more like I've met a soul mate.

Evelyn calls us in to eat. They asked me by phone what my food preferences were. I said, "Authentic Colombian food." She serves us a plate of typical *arroz con pollo*, rice mixed with shredded chicken, fried plantains, *bollo* (a corn roll), and salad. Jose, his parents, and I sit at the table, set for four.

"Evelyn, aren't you going to join us?"

"I ate earlier."

I remember this custom: the woman of the house stands by as guests eat. Evelyn's mother doesn't join us either but spends the evening watching vintage Mexican movies on TV.

After dinner, we return to the front terrace. Miguel Ángel puts on his bright yellow soccer shoes and runs to the field to join his team. We share more stories, until I notice Jose's parents getting restless. I consult with Jose, and he calls a cab. We'll meet on Saturday to do some sightseeing if he can change his shift at work as a security guard. We exchange email addresses and phone numbers.

The Wi-Fi reception at the hotel is irregular, so I call Jose on his cell phone the next day. He's at work. "Madrina, two of my coworkers are sick, so I can't get Saturday off to spend with you. I'm so sorry."

I'm terribly disappointed. The realization of how fond I am of him takes me by surprise.

"And Sunday?" I ask.

"I work half a day."

"I'd like to take you all out for dinner."

We agree that I'll go to his house Sunday afternoon, my last day.

Facing a Saturday with no plans, I arrange with a guide to go bird watching at a national park. I sleep poorly, beleaguered by itching insect bites.

Sunday afternoon. Jose, Evelyn, Miguel Ángel, and Kevin, freshly showered, hair still damp, are waiting for me. They want to show me their neighborhood. We walk the narrow streets, past neighbors chatting on their front patios. Ah, yes. *This* is the Barranquilla I remember: streets alive with voices of family and friends and loud strains of coastal music pouring from houses, corner shops, and restaurants. And I, too, am with family.

After a few blocks, we reach a main street and a mall. I realize this is what they want to show me. We tour the mall, stop for lemonade, and head to a large area with rides and games for kids. I buy the boys some tickets, and they race off. We laugh, watching them chasing each other in bumper cars. They hook me into playing a shuffleboard game. We pose for more photos, one of me with each of them, and then all together. They want to eat at the food court and all know exactly what to order.

While we eat, it starts to rain. The wind whips the tree branches into a frenzy. Then the deafening rolls of thunder. A wild tropical storm, like the many I weathered in the past—now, on my last night. Lightning strikes, and the lights go out in the mall. We've come unprepared for the rain and all squeeze into a taxi for the short ride home.

We watch the rain through the open door of the house, while Jose tells me of his struggle to educate his children. Before he took his job as a security guard, he worked for eight years in a coal mine in the Guajira, the northeastern corner of Colombia, close to Venezuela.

"What did you do there?" I ask.

"I checked the quality of the coal. I came home every eight days."

I wonder if that was under- or aboveground, picturing his thin figure covered with coal dust in a deep, dark tunnel. I hope it was the latter.

He is happy with his job now, he tells me, and works overtime, sometimes twelve-hour shifts, in order to get ahead.

If only I could stop the clock and make these fleeting moments last—but when the rain lets up, I ask them to get me a taxi. "I must be up early for my flight tomorrow." Evelyn goes off to look for a cab and returns ten minutes later with a taxi, but not the reliable neighborhood driver they hoped for. They are not comfortable entrusting me to this strange man.

The entire family—sons, daughters, son-in-law, granddaughter, and mother-in-law—gathers to say goodbye. I hug them all. Just before getting into the cab, I turn to Jose and squeeze him tight one last time, burying my face into his neck.

It's not until the next morning that I see his email. "Madrina, please call and tell me that you arrived at the hotel safely. I am worried." I attempt to send him an email from the hotel and then from the airport but am unable to get an Internet connection.

Afterthoughts

Barranquilla is now a dream memory. I replay the scenes in my mind so as not to forget. Yet, unlike in the past five decades, I now have phone numbers and email addresses to maintain these renewed friendships.

I email Jose as soon as I arrive back in Chile. After two weeks of no response, I write to his son Kevin, "I'm worried. No news."

Jose writes a brief email the next day. His mother, Herminda, suffered a stroke and is hospitalized. "Madrina," he says, "we miss you. It seems we've known you for a long time. I was so sad when you left. . . . Couldn't find the words . . ."

His feelings reflect mine, I write. I send photos, more emails, but receive no more responses. Impatient, I call him. Hearing his voice, with its distinctive coastal accent, makes him a real, flesh-and-blood person again, not just a dream. His mother is now home and receiving therapy. On Sunday, all the family will celebrate her eighty-seventh birthday. They've even hired a mariachi band. "This may be her last birthday," he says.

Since my return, I've learned more about the man who is my godson. He is not proficient at the computer. Though his handwritten letters were always neat and grammatically correct, his typed emails are short and garbled yet reflect an openly affectionate person. I realize that he is a dedicated family man who works long hours and has little time to write or learn computer skills. Disappointed, I think at first I'll have to modify my expectations for communication. But soon we find that frequent phone calls work well. In each phone call and email, Jose showers me with multiple blessings. *Que Dios la bendiga*, Madrina.

I want to ease his load. I've offered to help with the

education of the two boys. Kevin graduates from high school and must decide on a future course of study, which will involve major expenses. We decide we'll go fifty-fifty.

"It's a loan," he says. "I'll pay you back when I can."

"No," I insist. "It's a sign of my affection for you."

My whirlwind visit to Barrio Las Américas left me dissatisfied. Barrio faces and scenes hold me in their grasp. I realize that I want to stay involved with that community. I have Agripina and Eugenia in mind and am exploring the possibility of a micro-loan project founded by returned Peace Corps volunteers to support small barrio business endeavors.

How can I *not* help?

XII. AMERICA REVISITED

Over one month, I journey across America, visiting four emblematic landscapes—New York, Washington, DC, the Midwest, and California—tasting their rich, varied geography, history, and culture. Seeing these places through the eyes of others—those of a son and good friends—sharpens my perceptions and appreciation for my homeland. I become a sponge, eager to absorb the scenes, the ideas, and the diversity swirling about me like brightly colored shards of glass in a kaleidoscope.

My New York State of Mind

First impression: the color green. Everywhere. Spring foliage shouting with its greenness, a refreshing change from the muted grays and browns of a drought-ridden city.

Commencement at Columbia University: a euphoric sea of powder blue–clad graduates and proud family members, including us. Nico has earned his master's of science degree specializing in sustainability management. The speeches encouraging graduates to "go forth and make this world a better place" speak to me. I feel a graduate again, eager to do grand things with my future. In October, I'll be attending the fiftieth reunion of my Berkeley class.

Metromania: When I descend the stairs into the mouth of the monster, the pervasive odor of metal, humidity, rotting garbage, and urine and the rhythmic *clackety-clackety-clack* of the trains invade my senses. Read the signs, find the blue line, the R car, "stand clear of the closing doors"; scramble out to find the red line; go up the stairs, across the hallway, down the uptown stairs to the opposite platform; wait for the number 2 express and watch for rats scouring the tracks; then transfer at Times Square to the yellow line, get off at Fourteenth Street, find the southwest exit. Uptown, downtown, across town, days of constant movement. At night, faint rumblings from that subterranean world ease us to sleep in our basement apartment.

Grand Central Station at 6:00 p.m.: a maze of humanity, a swarming anthill, crisscrossing, colliding, hurrying-scurrying. In the midst, a bewildered me searches for a US mailbox.

Garbage: Shocking, discouraging mountains of unrecyclable

garbage at Shake Shack, where we dine in Grand Central's food court. Add the garbage from the thousands of fast-food enterprises, and one wonders if home recycling can ever make a difference.

Parks: Central and Riverside Parks and community gardens—green, leafy gems inserted throughout the city providing respite to us, the dogs, the birds, and the squirrels. Blue jays, robin redbreasts, and bright cardinals treat us to their song.

A walk in the woods—in the city.

One Nation

We're on the road from New York City to Washington, DC. The passing landscape sparks talk of random bits of American history and geography. I'm with my thirty-eight-year-old son, Nico, born and raised in Chile, and Laura, his American girlfriend, a recent, sunny presence in his life. This is his first visit to the nation's capital, and he's eager to go. I am, too. It was his idea. I treasure this time with Nico, who's lived in New York for five years, and now I'll get to know Laura.

The freeway doesn't allow much of a view of Philadelphia. But then—"Look over there! Isn't that the tower of Independence Hall?" Even from a distance, I recognize the iconic spire rising above the surrounding buildings.

"Nico, that's where the Declaration of Independence was signed." He never studied American history. Unexpectedly, I have the opportunity to imbue him with a bit of his heritage.

An overhead freeway sign announces Betsy Ross Boulevard. "Do you know who she was?" I ask.

He doesn't. I tell the story of the first American flag.

"Do you know what the flag was made of?" he asks.

He has me there.

"Hemp."

"Really? How do you know?"

"I read it somewhere."

Upon arrival, we head for George Washington University and the closing session of the yearly Peace Corps Connect conference. Nico encouraged me to attend in order to receive an award for my memoir from the Peace Corps Writers. Amid the sea of gray heads, I spot two former Colombia Peace Corps colleagues. We hug and laugh at our changed appearances. We last saw each other fifty years ago. Nico and Laura listen to us reminisce about those days when we were young and adventuresome. I worry they'll be bored, but their laughter and intent expressions tell me they're not. Maybe Nico can see a bit of the twenty-year-old me through my seventy-three-year-old exterior.

The featured event, an onstage conversation between journalists Sarah Chayes and Sebastian Junger, captures the audience's complete attention as they discuss the prevalent alienation in our modern society. Junger refers to the culture shock Peace Corps volunteers experience upon returning to the United States. I nod in agreement. Mine lasted an entire year. He goes on to describe the difficulty that soldiers returning from combat have in adjusting back to our bitterly divided society, based on a culture of fame and greed. To be happy, he asserts, humans need to live in a cohesive community where they can feel needed. In the past, neighborhoods provided that sense of belonging, but now families live more and more in isolation. His proposals confirm what I've believed for years— that money is the predominant value in American society. Now, in 2016, I despair more than ever at the dismal prospect of reversing this wave of materialism when a leading presidential candidate is a representative of gross consumption.

As we file out of the lecture hall, the audience is strangely quiet, perhaps contemplating Junger's concluding message: "Can we save ourselves?"

At an outdoor wine reception, I tell Nico and Laura, "Come. I want you to meet an old friend."

"Nico and Laura, meet Denny."

They shake hands, and Nico says, "My mom tells me you were a photographer in Vietnam."

"Yeah, I was. Immediately after returning to the States from Colombia, I was drafted. Direct from the Peace Corps into the Army."

"No kidding! What happened with all your photos?"

"The Army kept most of them."

I sense that Denny doesn't want to go into Vietnam details, and we turn to memories of our Colombian exploits.

Sunday, our only day for sightseeing. A glorious day in my nation's capital, a nation in which I haven't resided for over four decades. Is this patriotism that I'm feeling, this mix of nostalgia and pride? I last visited Washington, DC, many years ago. Today I feel like I'm seeing it for the first time, perhaps because I'm experiencing it through the eyes of my son as he first beholds this pulsing heart of the capital—its monuments, the National Mall, the Reflecting Pool, the round-domed Capitol, and the just inaugurated National Museum of African American History and Culture. The flags and monuments and museums remind me of the stories of this nation—its founding, growing pains, tragedies, errors, and triumphs.

We decide to start at the Capitol and walk the long, open vista to the Lincoln Memorial.

"Where shall we go first? There's so much to see." I say.

Immediately to our left stands the imposing National Native American Museum. "That seems like a good place to begin," offers Nico. "After all, they were here *first*. I've been reading about their sustainability practices."

To our surprise, the main exhibit features the cultures of

the Inca Trail, which extends the western length of South America, from Colombia to central Chile. An uncanny coincidence.

We wander through displays highlighting the accomplishments of the Inca people, admiring the rich colors of intricately woven textiles and stopping to study the details of the facsimile of a complex rope bridge used to cross deep canyons. But what catches my attention is the sacred Incan tradition of reciprocity (*ayni*) manifest in photographs of hillside communal agricultural terraces and marketplace activities. *Ayni*, I read, is the backbone of daily Incan human-to-human interaction, in which there is a mutual flow of giving and receiving. I am struck by how this concept dovetails with the ideas the two journalists put forth at the conference. I think about their argument that the alienation of individuals in our society has its roots in our lack of community, cooperation, and solidarity. A deeply unsettling picture.

These weighty thoughts percolate in my mind as we continue our stroll along the Mall to visit the United States Botanic Garden, where we pause to admire the visiting butterflies and unusual cactus flowers. Nico points out several native Chilean plants to Laura. I'm pleased to see that she shares this botanical interest with us.

Outside, map in hand, we identify one grand museum after another. Lacking sufficient time, we take a quick peek into the central hall of the Air and Space Museum, but a security guard shouts, "Either go through the security line or get out!" Welcome to the new America.

We come upon the open-air war monuments: World War II, the Korean and Vietnam Wars. Sobering reminders. My thoughts return to Sebastian Junger's analysis of returning soldiers' alienation in our deeply divided modern society, where they are unable to experience the sense of belonging that they lived when in active duty. I realize that this message of community and solidarity keeps surfacing again and again everywhere on this Washington sojourn.

Now, before us, the gleaming Washington Monument. I study the slim white obelisk rising into the intense blue sky. Bright, fluttering flags ring the monument. Just beyond rises the bronze-toned Museum of African American History and Culture. Barricades maintain order in the winding lines of opening-day visitors, whose bright faces reflect anticipation and pride. The air vibrates with rock music, while savory smells waft from soul-food kitchens.

The sun hangs low in the sky as we climb the marble stairs of the Lincoln Memorial. Standing before the solemn sculpture of Lincoln, I ponder the words of his Second Inaugural and Gettysburg Addresses inscribed on the walls. Again, war and injustice are the focus. I'm impressed how relevant his words are today, still here for thousands to read, urging us to reflect upon injustices, like those caused by slaveowners "wringing their bread from the sweat of other men's brows." A familiar phrase I memorized in school stands out: "With malice toward none, with charity for all . . ."

From his grand marble chair, Lincoln has a view across the Reflecting Pool to the new Museum of African American History and Culture. But his countenance is lined with worry. Does he despair that our nation hasn't followed his counsel that "a house divided against itself cannot stand"?

Heartland, USA

"I see everything through new eyes now that I know you're coming," writes my friend Ann. She's invited me to visit her in Osage, Iowa, her husband's hometown, where she spends summers, escaping Chilean winters.

In 1951, when I was nine years old, I drove with my parents across the country for a month in our gray Plymouth, my only previous experience in the Midwest. Reading the Burma Shave signs posted on fences along the flat cornfields is my strongest memory.

Iowa. Let's see. Where's that? I go to Google Maps. There— just south of Minnesota, west of Wisconsin and Illinois, north of Missouri, and east of Nebraska and South Dakota. A closer look at the map reveals names that evoke tales I read as a child, sagas of explorers and fur trappers and homesteaders: Grand Junction, Sioux City, Marquette, Council Bluffs, Des Moines. I've been doing some reading to get myself into a Midwest frame of mind. In *Main-Travelled Roads*, Hamlin Garland describes with bitterness turn-of-the-nineteenth-century farm life as endless drudgery and privations but whose actors prepared the way for future generations of farm families. Carol Bodensteiner, in *Growing Up Country: Memories of an Iowa Farm Girl*, depicts the challenges and hard work of 1950s Iowa farm life and its traditions—Sunday chicken dinners, farm hospitality—that exemplify the values underlying so much of American culture.

Flying into Minneapolis from New York, I scan the Minnesota landscape. No wonder it's called the Land of a Thousand Lakes. Ann and I meet at the airport, where she's reserved a rental car. We have a three-hour drive ahead of us, including giving a ride home to Ann's friend, eighty-nine-year-old Betty. It's 5:00 p.m., and none of us has had lunch, so we stop at Perkins road-side restaurant. FREE SLICE OF PIE EVERY MONDAY, announces a sign in the window. Today is Monday. The out-of-breath waitress explains she's just returned from bringing their quarter horses home from a show where her daughter competed. She shows us photos on her cell phone.

I order an omelet, which comes with sides of salad, french fries, and a "mammoth muffin." Actually, all the servings are mammoth. We each leave with a slice of pie in a plastic box. Mine is berry.

Ann turns off the highway onto a gravel road leading to Betty's farmhouse, a neat, yellow, two-story wooden structure, set in a grove of trees. My first Iowa farmhouse. Cornfields stretch out on both sides. Betty invites us into the spacious kitchen and offers us a glass of milk. Her daughter, who lives down the road, comes by. She offers us brownies. They talk about the serious flooding from days ago and how much the "crick" rose.

I ask Betty's daughter, "Do you have a farm, too?"

"We have acreage," she replies.

Later I ask Ann, "What's the difference between acreage and a farm?" She doesn't know, but eventually I learn that one depends for one's livelihood on a "farm." Not so with "acreage."

Betty hugs Ann and me goodbye with directions to drive to the blacktop, pass through the town of Lake Mills, and then left, back to Highway 35.

We continue south, an orange sun sinking below the horizon on our right. It's dark when Ann turns off the highway.

"This should be Highway 9."

An empty blackness envelops us. No lights. Just a straight, narrow, dark road.

Ann says, "Do you think we're headed east?"

"I have no idea, Ann! You're the one who's been here before!"

"But I've never driven it at night. We'll just have to stay on this road until we come to a town."

Finally, the lights of the town of Manly come into view. We're on the road to Osage.

Osage. The City of Maples. Population: 3,500. Main Street.

We pull up in front of a Subway sandwich shop, next door to the pink-and-white neon sign of the Watts movie theater. To the left of the Subway shop, Ann inserts a key to open a narrow brown door. Up a flight of red stairs, we enter the small apartment, which was home to Ann's husband and his five cousins, who had tragically lost their parents.

I look around. The differing wallpaper patterns in each room and faded upholstery peeking out from under brightly patterned quilts (Ann's touch) speak of the passing of years, yet it's as if the inhabitants have just stepped out for a while. Everywhere, family belongings seem to have their stories to tell: pillowcases with embroidered flowers on my bed, poodle-dog bedside lamps, shelves of old encyclopedias and *Reader's Digest*s, framed, embroidered biblical inspirations, elaborate vases with artificial flowers, a claw-foot bathtub, a roomy kitchen.

The next day dawns cool and windy. We take a stroll around town, visiting the library and the courthouse. Ann invites me to a gathering of the Alpha writing group at Margaret's house. Several have recently published books. I get my first exposure to jokes about Minnesotans (as told by Iowans).

"What do Minnesotans call pretty girls?"

"Visitors."

"What's the best thing coming out of Minnesota?"

"Highway I-35."

Later, I hear Minnesotans telling the same joke about Iowa.

Ann has planned a trip east through Decorah, Iowa, and then on to Wisconsin and her hometown of Richland Center. Just past the Osage outskirts stretch flat corn- and soybean fields, punctuated by neat white farmhouses and barns.

"I just can't believe you're really here!" Ann says. We've talked for years about visiting each other's hometowns. She slows down for me to snap photos of farms, barns, and silos. She wants me to have a complete Midwest experience. We are on the lookout for colorful examples of barn quilts painted on barn sides. Big green-and-yellow John Deere harvesters chug along the rows.

I feel stupid asking, but I must. "Why are the corn stalks so brown?"

"It's not corn for eating. It's used for animal feed and fuel production."

As we near Decorah, the flat landscape rises into rolling hills. Highway cuts reveal cliffs of exposed yellow limestone. We meet Cindy, a niece of Ann's husband, for lunch and a tour of the highlights of the area, including the famous Decorah eagles' nest, whose activities Santiago streams live on his computer in Chile. This late in the year, the nest is empty, aside from the cameras. I send him a photo, asking, "Any messages for your eagle friends?"

"You're really there?" he texts back. He thinks I'm kidding. Yet I must keep repeating to myself, *I am really here*—not only at the site of the Decorah eagles, but *in Iowa with Ann*. So often we've talked of such a visit, but somehow it always seemed a pipe dream. But we made it happen.

In another hour, I catch my first glimpse since childhood of the mighty Mississippi, still heavy with last week's floodwaters. Across the bridge, a sign welcomes us to Wisconsin, America's Dairyland. As I gaze out at the lush, green landscape, a small kernel of something about Wisconsin surfaces from deep in my memory: a book I read years ago . . . *A Sand County Almanac*. That's it! Isn't that set in Wisconsin? Ann hasn't heard of it. Now, who was the author? Aldo something.

Edie, a family friend of Ann's, is expecting us in her Richland Center home. Dinner talk centers on Edie's friendship with Lana Peters, Svetlana Alliluyeva, Stalin's daughter, who spent her final years here. Edie shows us her Lana memorabilia: newspaper articles and notes from her. I'm fascinated. I've recently read *Stalin's Daughter*, by Rosemary Sullivan, who visited our writing group last summer in Chile. Then there's the connection with architect Frank Lloyd Wright, who was born in Richland Center and whose top architect married Svetlana. Seeing my interest, Edie gives me her copy of *Loving Frank*, a novel by Nancy Horan based on Mamah Borthwick's tragic love affair with Wright.

I ask Edie if she's heard of *A Sand County Almanac*.

"Of course! Written by Aldo Leopold."

"And isn't it set in Wisconsin?"

"It is. He was from Baraboo, not far from here."

I want to know more and turn to Google. Sure enough. The book came out in 1949, after Leopold died, but since then has sold over two million copies. He is now considered the father of today's environmental movement. Wow.

The next day, we set off to see the sights of Ann's hometown: her family home and her grandparents', her church and school, an old warehouse designed by Frank Lloyd Wright. Outside town, we wind through green hills and valleys to Oakwood

Fruit Farm, set among apple orchards. Autumn is in the air. I snap photos of bright pumpkin and gourd displays and buy a black-and-white photo of an American eagle for Santiago.

Following lunch at the Empire Grill in downtown Richland Center, we embark on a town tour of historic Victorian homes set in the midst of wide green lawns. Lon, a local history buff, takes us around in his red Jeep convertible. He, Edie, and Ann name almost every family that used to live or still lives in the houses we pass. Edwards. Clausius. Brock. Demmer, Turner . . .

"How did you know so many people?" I ask Ann.

"My dad had a business here, where I'd help out. . . . In a small town, many people stay."

We must return to Osage tonight, and at Prairie du Chien (love that name), once again we cross the two branches of the Mississippi. Somewhere along the empty, straight highway bordered by cornfields, a highway patrol car coming in the opposite direction flashes its bright lights.

"That's for me," says Ann, as she pulls over to the shoulder.

"How do you know?"

"I was speeding."

The Iowa Highway Patrol officer asks for her license. "You were driving sixty-nine miles per hour in a fifty-five zone."

"I got distracted watching the beautiful sunset," says Ann.

He writes out the ticket, fudging a bit on her actual speed to lessen the fine. "You've got to watch for deer crossing at this hour."

Ann turns serious, keeping her eyes on the speedometer. "That was my first ticket in my whole driving life." I can't resist laughing. We reach Osage four hours later.

Osage's Main Street is decorated with long husks of corn tied to streetlamp posts. Harvest smells and football fever fill the air. It's homecoming weekend. Probably is in towns all across the country. "Go Green Devils" in bright paint splashes across Osage store windows.

Ann and I take to the road again back to Decorah to attend homecoming weekend at her alma mater, Luther College. We spot an A&W Root Beer sign and pull over. Wow, when was the last time . . . ? We order the full Monty: hamburgers, fries, and milk shakes. I want to experience America's heartland to the fullest. I snap photos of murals depicting 1950s scenes of smiling A&W waitresses and families. I notice there's not a dark face among them.

Ann is eager to show me the campus and introduce me to friends. She says to all, "This is her first time in the Midwest."

"Welcome to the Corn State!"

"Is it what you expected?"

"Better!" I say.

Our day is filled with magnificent musical performances by the college's five choirs, symphonic orchestra (whose "Star-Spangled Banner" brings a lump to my throat), and concert band. The quiet campus, set amid lush green hills, presents a vivid contrast with my Berkeley alma mater.

The following day at dusk, under the mantle of a mauve-and-blue sky, an eyelash of a moon winking at us, we return to Osage. I can make out the shadowy contours of barns, round-domed silos, dark trees clustered around farmhouses and lit-up harvesters still at work. In the distance blink the tiny red lights of wind turbines. Ann points out the lights of an Amish buggy on the roadside. We agree that the strong stench in the air must be hogs.

Back in Osage, we head across the street to the Flat Pie and Red Eye Grill, the only option at this hour. Our patty melts are scrumptious. Ann asks to meet the chef. A young man comes out from the kitchen.

"Wow!" says Ann. "Where did you learn to cook like that?"

"Pretty much taught myself," he replies.

"What's your name?"

"Dakota. I have a twin named Shiloh."

"Are you here every day?"

"I work here after school."

"What are your plans after high school?"

"I want to join the army."

"Why?"

"Want to serve my country."

A pretty young redhead sweeping the floor comes up to Ann and says in a soft voice, "I heard you mention Chile. You're the owners of that apartment above the Subway, aren't you? I'm Brianna. I think I'm related to you."

After a few questions, Ann concludes that her husband's stepmother is Brianna's great-grandmother.

My last full day in Osage. We grab a sandwich at the Subway shop, where everyone knows each other. We bump into Ramona from the Alpha writing group. As we leave, Red, a bearded Subway regular, nods in our direction. "Yous guys have a good one."

Out on Main Street, huge feed and grain trucks roar past us, trailer trucks haul tractors, a massive big rig advertises Frito-Lay. The plaintive moan of a train strikes a nostalgic chord within me. *Whoo-whoo. Whoo-whoo.* America at work. Walt Whitman's "I Hear America Singing" comes to mind.

Ann drives through town, stopping for me to take photos of the trees. In just one week, their leaves have turned bright yellow and scarlet. For my final outing, we head east once more, to a sign we saw indicating Hayden Prairie Reserve.

"I want to set my eyes on *real* prairie grass," I tell Ann. We turn left just beyond the town of Saratoga, following ruler-straight roads. Unexpectedly, we come upon the town of Lime Springs, set amid wide expanses of cornfields.

To a local I say, "The towns seem to be equidistant from each other."

"That's right. These towns started as rest and supply stops for covered wagons. Twenty miles were about as far as they could travel in a day."

We ask for directions and soon arrive at the reserve. It's not what I expected. The word "prairie" conjures up endless stretches of long, soft, waving grass. We follow a little-used trail into tall brown brush and brambles, dotted with wild blue asters. In photographs taken in spring, I see a green landscape populated with a variety of wildflowers. I snap photos, but they cannot capture the landscape. An information sign tells us that this 240-acre plot is one of the few remnants of tall prairie grass that once covered most of Iowa. Upon the invention of the steel plow, Iowa's countryside was converted into farmland. I try to imagine wagon trains making their way through this thick, prickly bracken. I wonder if we saw remnants of prairie grass on our family cross-country trip in '51. I doubt we took notice.

Rain and gray skies greet us in the morning as we head north to Minneapolis, where Ann will drop me off at the airport for my final destination on this journey: California and my hometown. I give her a hug. "Okay, Ann, now it's your turn to visit me."

California Dreamin'

Though it's been only a year, the uniqueness and wonders of this landscape surprise me. I notice cultural differences between Chile and California; I'm reminded of things forgotten; I renew friendships and my love affair with this place. I'm struck by the novel, the creative, the humorous.

Things I Notice

A former male classmate, whom I haven't seen in years, shakes my hand in greeting. So accustomed am I to Chilean cheek-kissing society, hand shaking feels stiff and formal. I wonder if he thinks I'm forward when I greet him with a hug and peck on the cheek.

The sex-change process is now referred to as gender reassignment. Terminology related to this topic is clearly adapting to the politically correct.

Baseball can be exciting, especially if the San Francisco Giants are playing (and winning) the World Series.

To this city dweller, the abundance of wildlife is a delight: frisky squirrels, noisy blue jays, and shiny, coal-black crows harvesting the abundant acorns.

The neighbor's goats, Buff and Sunny, crunch on dry magnolia leaves as if they were potato chips. Goat petting leaves the scent of goat cheese on my hands all day.

The vegetation in the Fairfax hills varies according to its orientation: pungent redwood, madrone, bay and dry grass each mark their territory with their distinctive scent.

I never tire of the ferry trip across the bay to San Francisco, a city that always surprises. Today a guitarist plays for money by the line for the San Francisco cable car. His T-shirt reads: LEGAL-IZE GAY MARIJUANA. Love it.

Euphoric Moments

At the Muir Beach lookout, I long to soar like the snow-white gulls over the shimmering Pacific. The endless expanse of air and sea before me fills my spirit.

As I hike along the Sky Oaks Trail in the Fairfax hills, my olfactory receptors detect an unmistakable scent. I'm standing in a field of Chilean tarweed, their tiny yellow flowers winking in the sunlight. It is unclear whether the original habitat of this lowly, fragrant ground cover is Chile or California.

A flying sensation wafts through me as I cross the Richmond–San Rafael Bridge over the San Francisco Bay. From its silken surface, tiny, sun-struck wavelets sparkle like fallen stars.

Surprises

A covey of wild turkeys grazes in a field by Spirit Rock. I don't remember seeing them when I lived here.

Our car headlights illuminate two antlered deer crossing the road in the black night.

A childhood playmate relates the story of our adventurous ride down my steep road on our red scooters, a ride that ended in screams and crashes when a long snake crossed our path.

Out for a stroll, I discover a Little Free Library on a pole—a small, red, wooden house with shelves of books—on Sycamore Avenue. I drop off a book I no longer need.

I'm still capable of reaching the top of Mt. Tamalpais on foot.

Yapa

San Anselmo Avenue. I walk the familiar few blocks of shops, along one sidewalk and across the street to the other. I imagine that Ann is with me. What things would she notice in my home-town? That, unlike the straight Iowa roads, the street curves following the course of the creek? That the facades of some build-ings look old, late nineteenth century, as in Osage? I'd take her to the two bridges that cross the creek so she'd see that the shops on the street's east side are built out on pilings over the creek. I'd tell her that the tame-looking creek can transform into a roaring torrent in heavy rains, flooding downtown and creekside neigh-borhoods. She might notice several empty storefronts and the 1950s constructions that house beauty and home décor shops, consignment stores, and restaurants. She couldn't help but see the solid row of parked cars blemishing the small-town land-scape. Or the cyclists sitting outside the coffee shops. Or the dog bowls with water in retail doorways. I'd point out Booksmith, the tiny bookshop I frequent, and the Carnegie library, where I used to check out books from the Children's Room.

I've always referred to San Anselmo as a "small town," but I realize that size is relative. With Osage, Iowa, in my head, I see this place with new eyes. Though San Anselmo's population hasn't grown much over the years, a constant stream of traffic flows along its main artery, Sir Francis Drake Boulevard, head-ing to nearby towns. For that reason, San Anselmo used to be known as the Hub.

If my oldest hometown friend, Paula, were with me this morning, we might begin our day with brunch at Hilda's Cof-fee Shop. I'd remind her that my father was a regular here.

Then we'd stroll down the street and reminisce. *Remember the Ben Franklin five-and-dime, where we'd buy our school supplies? That store there used to be the Home Market. Here was Rossi's Pharmacy. But the old barbershop is still here, and Ludwig's Liquors, Jack's Drugstore, and the brick Wells Fargo Bank. Too bad the bakery's gone.* From the bridge we'd see the marquis, all that remains of the Tamalpais Theater, on Drake Boulevard. *That's where we cried over Elvis Presley crooning "Love Me Tender."*

"Home county" is perhaps a better choice of words than "hometown," because San Anselmo's limits spill over into other small towns. If Ann were here, I'd take her west through Fairfax, Lagunitas, San Geronimo, and Woodacre, towns that follow the creek, into Marin County's dairy-farm country, which is the route Paula and I will take today.

Noontime. I pick up Paula, and we drive to Pt. Reyes Station, a small agricultural community. Dark clouds are gathering. The wind carries the scents of hay and horses and cows. Toby's Barn is a must for checking out local produce: tomatoes and squash, honey, jams, cheeses. We head to the Station House Café, where we used to go with our mothers for a yearly mother-daughter lunch. It's still one of our regular stops. For dessert, we cross the street, following tantalizing scents to the Bovine Bakery. It starts to rain, and the warm space seems like a good place to be. But soon it's closing time, and a white-aproned employee asks Paula to flip the OPEN sign in the window to CLOSED, while assuring us that we can hang out for a while. Three customers besides us remain: two very wet cyclists, Michelle from Ireland and Len, whom she met on the road, and Dorsey, a ranger from Point Reyes National Seashore. Both cyclists are traveling from the Canadian to the Mexican border.

We exchange names. Paula introduces me to everyone we

encounter with the same fanfare: "This is my friend from South America. Suzie and I grew up here, but she lives in Chile and comes here every year."

We ply the cyclists for details of their travels while nibbling on our pastries and sipping coffee. Where did you start? How long have you been on the road?

"I visited Chile," says Michelle, "as translator for a group studying receding glaciers."

Paula mentions that I recently published a memoir. Michelle is interested. She's keeping a blog on this trip and plans to write a book.

Small, gray-haired Dorsey, who has been silent until now, joins the conversation. "I was in the Peace Corps."

"Really? Where?" I say.

"In Greece."

"I'm just coming from the yearly conference for returned volunteers." I thrive on these wonderful connections that appear in unexpected places and times.

"What do you do now?"

"I used to work at a lot of men's jobs, like driving heavy machinery. For a while, I piloted a helicopter. I'm a local and now work as park ranger. Every year I organize a group of California-returned Peace Corps volunteers to help out at the park, clean trails and such."

The rain lets up. Dusk is just around the corner. The cyclists will head to a nearby campground. Michelle says she'll buy my book and read it in her tent at night. We smile for photos, arms linked like old friends, and say our goodbyes.

Saturday morning. I meet up with friends on the terrace of the Coffee Roasters: Lindsey and her husband, my former classmate,

Malcolm, and two other classmates, Joe and Melodie. We talk about kids and grandkids living on the East Coast. I ask Joe how his books are progressing. He says he's thinking of self-publishing. I mention that I'm working on a new book, a collection of essays similar to those inserted between each chapter in my memoir. This reminds Lindsey of the New Orleans Creole word *lagniappe*, meaning "a little something extra."

"That sounds like the Spanish word the barrio kids used in Colombia," I say. "When they'd see me heading for town, they'd call, "*Traigame la* ñapa—bring me a little gift." It must be the same word."

It's Fleet Week on the San Francisco Bay. As in other years, Paula and I drive up to the Marin County hills west of the Golden Gate Bridge to view the air show of the Blue Angels, the US Navy's acrobatic team. The day is bright and unusually hot. I'd like Ann to see this—the hills plunging toward the deep azure ocean, the Golden Gate Bridge spanning the bay, dotted with tiny white sails, and San Francisco, gleaming in the distance. The acrobatics over, we drive down to Rodeo Beach to inhale salty sea air. Sunbathers are folding their umbrellas and gathering towels, buckets, and spades.

"Suzie! Is that a coyote walking along the beach?" Paula asks.

"It sure looks like it. Look how it strolls among the bathers!" I've read of many coyote sightings in the county and warnings not to feed them. That wild creatures—coyotes, foxes, squirrels, raccoons, deer—make their home here is a continuous source of delight for me.

All this—easy access to the bridge, the bay, the sea air, the wildlife—is a part of my "home county" package and a gaping hole in my big-city days in Chile, where I must travel considerable distances to inhale a sea breeze or walk through a forest.

Another day, we drive the curving road up to Lake Laguni-tas to enjoy the heavenly scent of redwoods. Along the way, we encounter two young fawns. "Somewhere I read that does often give birth to twins," I tell Paula.

Farther along, she points toward a grassy pasture. "Look! Wild turkeys!"

We stand by the shimmering lake, listening to the birds, and then look up upon recognizing the call of a red-tailed hawk. Paula calls in response, "Caw, caw, caw."

The hills cast long shadows as we head back down into the town of Fairfax, where we stop for dinner at the Barefoot Café and ice cream at the Scoop. I scan the crowded window of the Fairfax Variety for grandchildren gifts.

I head back to the San Anselmo Coffee Roasters to meet with my friend Martha. I spot Lindsey on the terrace. We hug, and she says, "Martha's inside."

"Oh. You know Martha?"

"We go to the same church."

I'm beginning to feel like a local.

This year, I'm staying with my friend Donna. She worked at the Ross Valley Nursery School years ago, when my mother was the director.

"Would you like to visit the nursery school?" she asks. "Two teachers who knew your mother still work there."

They're surprised and pleased to see me.

"You have your mother's eyes."

"Doesn't she look like Jean?"

"She was wonderful with the kids."

"So elegant and professional."

Tears threaten. This place was an important part of my mother's life. Now it's a treat to be with women who knew her. They proudly show me the improvements they've made. I ask to go outside to visit the Secret Garden, a fairy-size plot of flowers, moss, and stepping-stones dedicated to my mother and her assistant director, Marge.

Donna and I meet with Paula for dinner. Donna moved south to San Diego for a few years to be near her daughters and grandkids, but she returned to Marin County last year.

"Why did you come back?" I ask her.

"Well, one of my daughters moved to Fairfax. And in San Diego I didn't have the connections I have here."

She and Paula talk about several local Italian families they know in common. Then she spots a former student at the next table and goes to talk to him. I watch with envy, remembering that years ago my mother often encountered former students or their mothers.

This must be what Sebastian Junger, the journalist at the Peace Corps convention, meant by "community."

In my little red rental, I head to the cemetery with flowers and clean the weeds from around my parents' grave. It is quiet up here on this hill, with just the rustling of the wind in the eucalyptus branches and the *knock-knock-knock* of the red-crested woodpeckers. Deer graze on the grass below.

I've decided I need a smaller suitcase. I'm not able to handle the large size anymore, so I head for the mall. Macy's has a luggage sale. While I'm here, might as well buy a couple of bras. In the lingerie department, a young woman helps me find what

I want among the dizzying maze of racks. Her name tag says JOCELYN. She speaks with a strong accent. I'm curious.

"Where are you from?"

"Haiti," she replies.

"How long have you been here?"

"Twenty-four years."

"I live in Chile," I say.

"I know the Chilean National Anthem." She starts humming. I hum along with her. "But how . . ."

"In Haiti I went to a private school. Its name was the Republic of Chile."

My last day. It's raining. The pungent scent of wet sycamore leaves on the pavement evokes childhood rainy days. Through the window, I see a blue jay perched on a telephone wire, acorn in its beak. I can just make out Red Hill through the mist.

In the afternoon, Paula and I take in a movie and dinner. It's time to say goodbye. We hug each other long and tight.

"You're my true soul sister, Suzie," she says. Only people who have known me since childhood call me Suzie. She is my deepest connection to this place.

I head back to Donna's in the damp, drizzly dusk. Lights in houses glitter in the gloom. Donna is away tonight. Her house will be dark. I suddenly feel very alone. In this place that once was home, I have no warm, welcoming family to go to.

I feel the rush as the airplane accelerates and lifts off the tarmac. In the early morning, we'll land in Santiago. My Santiago will be there waiting for me. I pull my journal from my backpack to read my impressions of this journey across America. A pattern of connecting threads unfolds before me: journalist

Sebastian Junger's exploration of man's need for a sense of belonging and community; the Incan core value of *ayni,* reciprocity; the generosity shown to me in all the homes in which I stayed across the country—New York, Washington, DC, Iowa, Wisconsin, and California; the discovery of the word *lagniappe, la* ñapa, the small gift offered freely. Chileans use the Quechua word, *yapa.* I love how this concept of generosity has taken root all over the Americas.

Community. Tribe. Family. In Chile I've had to build new communities, create new ties, but, like sea coral, they're layered on top of older, deeper connections. Internet and yearly trips to California have allowed me to reinforce my old ties with classmates, childhood friends, and former Peace Corps colleagues. My communities are not totally separate; their boundaries are porous. It's the connections and reciprocity among them that give richness and a sense of wonder to my days. *Yapa* offerings.

ACKNOWLEDGMENTS

Writing these essays has been a journey of self-discovery. Pointing me in the right direction, editor Annie Tucker pushed me to dig deeper and explore further to uncover essential lessons and insights. I am indebted to my colleagues of the Santiago Writers for their patience, encouragement, and sharp critiquing skills, especially to Danette Beavers, who knows that quotation marks follow punctuation. I thank my husband, Santiago, for his patience and understanding during the many hours I've spent at the computer. I must also express my gratitude to Peter Mark Roget, the author of the first modern-day thesaurus, without which I'd have been banging my head against a wall during this process.

My roots penetrate deep into two lands, California and Chile—their peoples, their cultures, and their landscapes. Each has contributed to the shape my immigrant life has taken.